FICTION IS FOLKS

Other books by the
same author:

A Day No Pigs Would Die
Path of Hunters
Millie's Boy
Soup
Fawn
Wild Cat
Bee Tree (poems)
Soup and Me
Hamilton
Hang for Treason
Rabbits and Redcoats
King of Kazoo (a musical)
Trig
Last Sunday
The King's Iron
Patooie
Soup for President

Eagle Fur
Trig Sees Red
Basket Case
Hub
Mr. Little
Clunie
Soup's Drum
Secrets of Successful Fiction
Trig Goes Ape
Soup on Wheels
Justice Lion
Kirk's Law
Trig or Treat
Banjo
Soup in the Saddle
The Seminole Seed
Fiction Is Folks

FICTION IS FOLKS

How to Create Unforgettable Characters

ROBERT NEWTON PECK

Writer's
Digest
Books

Cincinnati, Ohio

Library of Congress Cataloging in Publication Data
Peck, Robert Newton.
    Fiction is folks.

    Includes index.
    1. Fiction—Technique. 2. Chraracters and chaacteristics in literature. I. Title.
PN3383.C4P42   1983   808.3   83-10205
ISBN 0-89879-113-8

Design by Maria Carella

Foreword

I've known Robert Newton Peck for more than forty years, ever since we hunted frogs together in the Adirondacks, and he still surprises me, as he always has.

Rob is the author of *A Day No Pigs Would Die*, a fine and sensitive book for people of all ages. He also has written practically a whole library of books for young people that millions of kids, including my grandchildren, read with enthusiasm all by themselves, without being told to do so by an adult. Some of his books have been turned into highly successful television programs. Beyond that, Rob writes songs that make me laugh and tells jokes that make me cry.

Rob Peck also has the curious habit of wearing cowboy clothes, not in the West, where he rarely hangs out, but in Florida, on Madison Avenue, and on college campuses. He's so tall and lean that he looks great in his cowboy rig, and I admire his defiance of local customs.

Rob's first text on writing, *Secrets of Successful Fiction*, was both charming and professional.

While working on this second textbook on writing, he continued to be an individualist. When most writers succumb to the temptation to write books on how to write, they are intimidated by the standards, real or imagined, of *The New Yorker* magazine and the *New York Times* book section. As one can judge from his title, *Fiction Is Folks*, Rob marches to a different drum. His down-to-earth approach to the problems of writing fiction may startle some, but maybe it's time for a teacher of writing to take the monocle out of his eye, don a ten-gallon hat, and tell some down-home truths about spinning a yarn.

This is one textbook on writing that is actually fun to read, and part of the excitement is in disagreeing violently with some of Rob's more extreme statements. Beneath all his jokes is Rob's shrewd understanding of how to write sentences that people will enjoy reading. I cussed some of his pronouncements, but I think I learned a few things that will make me less inclined to be stuffy.

Anyone who wants to write for publication will find a lot of good advice, as well as some delightfully outrageous opinions, in *Fiction Is Folks*.

—SLOAN WILSON

Sloan Wilson is the author of *The Man in the Gray Flannel Suit, A Summer Place,* and a dozen other bestselling novels.

Contents

FICTION IS FOLKS

Up Front

Fiction is folks.

Here's proof. My dear friend and professional associate, Mr. Squire Rushnell, recently made a speech to about 150 aspiring writers. Every one of us listened.

Squire's job, up north in New York, is director of programming at the ABC television network. My three TV shows, *Soup and Me*, *Soup for President*, and *Mr. Little*, air on ABC.

"At ABC," Squire told us, "when we read scripts that are sent to us containing ideas for television shows, what we look for first is a *character*."

Mr. Budge Wallis, a vice-president at Writer's Digest Books, was also there. As we sat together, listening to Squire's good advice, Budge gave me a nudge. A professional jab, as his business is to publish books to help an emerging writer, like you, become a pro.

Fiction Is Folks was born.

Its purpose is to convince you that it is not plot, but *character*, that makes your story glisten.

"Hold it!" you may be saying. "I don't know any characters.

Do I find them in the Yellow Pages? Where do characters hang out?"

Fiction Is Folks will show you, chapter by chapter, how to flip over a rock and find folks for your fiction. How to recognize a character when you see him, or her, and then how to examine, calibrate, and hone a passel of personalities. After all, life is rife with people. They are your basic raw material.

This is my second book on writing.

My first, *Secrets of Successful Fiction*, was also published, in 1980, by Writer's Digest Books. Although that tiny text is chiefly a book on *style*, several of its chapters touch on characters and how they roll up their sleeves and work for you.

It's true.

My characters write my books.

People, not authors, determine a plot. Because authors aren't *in* books. Characters are. This point will be fully explained, and illustrated, in my chapter "Author . . . Butt Out."

I write this book with a smile.

Humor is the best tool of teaching. Too many textbooks are dull. Result? Teachers who use them can become dull. Since I like and respect teachers, this book's purpose is to help profs, as well as emerging authors, discover the fun of writing.

Education needs a face *lift*. A grin!

To become a memorable teacher, dear profs, don't be afraid to play the clown. I've learned more from clowns than I have from funeral directors—and so have you.

This book is a ham's circus, not a mortician's march. There's a laugh in every lesson. Honey, not vinegar. Not wine, but well-water from a farmer's bucket.

I believe in using my own work, my novels, to illustrate points for you to consider. Why? Because too many teachers preach theory, how-to-do-it maxims that they themselves have rarely inked into commercially published print.

So this is a how-Peck-does-it book.

It is fact. Not theory.

Accomplishment, even as limited as mine, beats theoretical how-to instruction. Pupils learn more from example than by rule. And seeing that the title of this book is *Fiction Is Folks*, I'm going to use folks to burn the lesson into your hide like a branding iron.

Another reason for my smile is that I just returned from Missouri, where I accepted one of the highest honors an American author can receive, the 1982 Mark Twain Award.

I won it for *Soup for President*.

No, that's wrong. I really didn't win the award. Soup did. And if you read my books about Soup, you'll see what a *character* he is.

Perhaps, someday in the future, *you'll* win the Mark Twain Award. If so, you will win it because of the *folks* in your fiction and for no other reason.

You'll win it because what readers often remember about a book is one wonderful character. Somebody so real, so close, that a reader wants that person as a friend—or a worthy opponent.

Readers are people.

Ergo, what interests people (and editors) most is other people, the ones that live in your pages.

Fiction Is Folks is not only a guide to characterization for an emerging writer. It's also a text for teachers. My purpose is not to bore but rather to excite, to agitate, and to goose. Writing is fun. If you don't agree, then perhaps you're in the wrong business. Writing is work, for sure. You must make it your hobby, your dreams, and your secret love.

Rapture in it.

The easiest way for this to happen is when you, the author, fall in love with a character and share him or her with a neighbor. A gift to a reader. Forget the royalties. Because, you see, it isn't your greed that creates your novel.

Your heart keeps only what it gives away.

1
Socrates and a Wide Receiver

Socrates was an ancient Greek who thought a lot.

As far as we know, Soc didn't play football. Nobody's perfect. Perhaps, had he played it, Socrates would have written fiction instead of philosophy.

Today, people read more fiction and watch more football than they read the writings of Socrates. There's a reason for this: Philosophy is dull; fiction and football are exciting.

Thinking, by itself, is not enough.

In a football game, Willie, who is a wide receiver, must not only think about the pass pattern that he is about to run; he also must execute it. Willie hears the quarterback's hut-hut-hut, slants in, head-fakes the cornerback, zigs out, and hauls in the pass.

Writing fiction is practicing the distinct difference between a thought and a thinker.

Thoughts have no flesh, no dimension, no color or texture, no smell, and no desire. But a *thinker*, even one of average intelligence like Willie, has all of those qualities and more. Willie thinks, talks, acts. If he fails to communicate and to act, Willie will sit out the game on a bench, just thinking.

On the bench is also where your writing will rest, until you realize that fiction is folks.

Fiction is Willie, age twenty-one, black.

It's also his respect for his coach, his desire to marry his girl, his love for his mother ("Hi, Mom!") and seven younger brothers and sisters. Their home is fatherless. Willie is their one hope for upward mobility, yet it all hinges on his football acumen and a pro contract.

Willie Ray Jefferson is not just number 88. He is a physical being, a fictional force. He's folks.

His knee hurts. Leaning over in the huddle, he feels volts of pain gnawing his entire leg, up his spine, making him bite his mouthpiece. Sweat smarts his eyes, yet the sweat comes not from the cold November afternoon. He missed most of last season because of knee surgery.

Willie is a liar.

He grins whenever Coach Burly asks about his knee and flashes him a thumbs-up sign. "Super," he lies. "Real decent. Stronger than ever." He tells the same lie to Ellie May, his girlfriend, who will marry him only if he makes the pros. She's pretty, knows it, and plans to marry well.

Today is Willie's final game as a senior at Indiana University. His grades, even in the mush courses, are fair to poor. This game is Willie's last chance. Somewhere, in one of the fifty thousand seats, sits a pro scout who came only to watch Willie Ray Jefferson catch a football.

"Fake 41 dive, red right square-in, on two."

Breaking from the huddle, Willie refuses to limp, fighting to ignore the screams from his knee, promising to ask the trainer to wrap it tighter, at the half. Cold numbs his fingers. One lonely snowflake dances between the twin bars of his facemask. Why, he asks himself, didn't I slap stickum on my hands? They feel dry. Footballs, in late November, are cannonballs.

Crowd noise blurs into his helmet. Only one sound matters . . . huts from a quarterback. A square-in pattern is what Willie fears most. He would fake straight ahead, as though running a fly; then cut left over the middle. Into the pit where the gorillas, the linebackers, prowl. On a third and seven, they would be backpedaling, expecting the pass.

The pro scout would be watching.

Willie Ray Jefferson envisions a short, squat man, with gray hair, an unlit cigar bulging one fat jowl, and a clipboard lying on his chubby knees, pencil poised, to check a star or an X beside the 88.

Split wide, Willie takes his upright stance, freezes, waits, watching the Ohio State cornerback creep in for the press, to get in the one legal bump to delay the pattern. His name is Leroy Lee, Willie knows, one hungry sophomore on two healthy legs. The kid mocks a grin at him.

"How's the knee, Jefferson? Hurting?"

Willie answers him. "Boy, you'll only see it from the back."

Hands on hips, Willie pauses, counting the huts, breaking on the second. Ducking the chuck, he cuts toward the middle where seven Ohio red jerseys are ready to converge. Don't look, he warns himself. Only the ball, the ball, the ball.

It comes.

The pass is high, a real leader. A hummer. A bullet that takes one second from passer to receiver. Arms extended, Willie stretches upward and out at a full run, leaping, leaving his body fully exposed, a target. As the ball's impact stings his hands, his eyes count the laces, about to hug it in.

For you, Mama, he thinks. You're home, watching my last game on the neighbor's TV, and this one's for . . .

His feet never touch the turf. The first hit, aimed at his head, tears off his helmet. The chinstrap rips. The second linebacker hits lower, knifing into his belly. Under the two of them, Willie goes down, holding the ball with both hands, hearing the snap of his knee and the shattering of pins and bone and tissue.

Then his pain.

He half hears whistles, crowd noise, and the male voice that drones on the IU stadium loudspeaker:

"First down . . . shaken up on the play . . ."

Shaken up? Willie Ray Jefferson cannot smile at the irony, hearing his knee explode, over and over, and yelling the burning words: No draft. No Steelers, no Saints, no Rams, no future, no nothing. And no Ellie.

"Don't move him."

A whiff stick has been cracked open and its acidic fumes torture his nose. Yet he cannot even move his head. Even the ground he lies on feels cold and numb, and Willie is little more than frozen mud, a run-over cat on fortune's highway. Black and white striped sleeves, and hands, try to pry the ball from Willie, without success. Time out is called. A stretcher comes and a band fills in to amuse the crowd.

Both ambulance doors bang closed and it is darker, yet the crowd noise stills and roars with each play. The game grinds on. Willie's game is over. At Bloomington Hospital, Willie sees a nurse's face look under his blanket at his knee and wince. But the she continues to chew her gum.

"How come," she asks him, "you're holding a football? Is that the winning ball or something?"

"No," Willie answers her. "I lost."

Now then, my dear and patient students, especially those of you who care little or naught for football . . . how dull indeed our story would be if we allowed our Willie only to think.

He thought, talked, acted.

We know what Willie Ray Jefferson believes in. And we can easily imagine the tender words he speaks to his mother, his brothers and sisters, and his girl. Earlier, we more or less agreed, thinking alone is not enough to sustain a story. Taking that a step further, neither is a combination of thought and talk.

Consider how you choose your closest friends.

Are they folks who only think and talk? They never *act?* If so, I rather pity you, for you're hanging out with a colorless crowd.

You expect your closest associates to *do* something. Maybe they don't *run* out on a football field to catch a pass; but they

(8)

run to catch a bus or a train. In fact, when you and your friend are talking on the telephone, he (or she) may terminate the chat by saying, "I'll talk to you tomorrow. I've got to *run*."

Remember this: A dull character, like a dull friend, is one who has all the mobility of a parking meter.

Readers choose books exactly the same way you select your sidekicks. The reader wants some action. So please do not *bench* your character. You, as an author, are also his coach, so whack his butt and send your hero smack out onto the field. Into the fray and frolic of activity.

When I came home from the war, from Europe, as a nineteen-year-old private, there was always one question that I heard from the folks back home:

"Rob, did ya see any *action?*"

I wasn't offended.

It really wasn't a question of gore. Merely one of humanity. It was just normal curiosity, wanting to know *what happened.*

As you mature into a professional writer, you will do well to study the way people really are. *Not* what they ought to be. This wee hunk of advice will speed your writing and hasten your success. Why? Because it's much easier to canoe downstream, not up.

Make sense?

It does for my dough. That's why writing a book like this one is so simple. Very, because all I have to do is tell you things you already know and have possibly forgotten or momentarily ignored. My job is not to make you play football. Instead, it is to tap your shoulder gently, to remind you of what *living* has already taught.

You and I are *alive.* We both bear the scars, and the scar tissue, to prove it. We've played the game.

I shall now end this chapter, because I have cogitated and chattered enough. If I continue to ramble on, you will continue to read, and you won't *do* anything yourself. At least the two of us now know the important difference between tepid philosophy and exciting, stadium-rousing fiction.

Philosophy is when you think about football. Fiction is when Willie Ray Jefferson plays it.

2
Peck Is a Character

I preached a sermon at our church.

My topic was "The Sanctity of Work."

As I was preparing it, our maid looked over my shoulder, eyeing my title with amusement. As almost every day I play golf, tennis, ride a horse, or take a nap, she suggested that I select a subject with which I was more familiar.

Nonetheless, I preached my magnificat. My opening blast to the congregation was as follows:

"Every man thinks three things about himself. One, that he is fantastic with the ladies. Two, that his life would make a seismic novel that only he himself could write. And thirdly, that, if asked, he could preach one crackerjack of a sermon."

I talked fifteen minutes.

Following my sermon, those few members of the congregation who had loyally remained apew to the very end, smiled dutifully, shook my hand, and forced themselves to say it was swell.

As an author, there's one more thing that I think about myself. That being, I make a dandy character in several of my books.

I put myself in them all the time.

This fetish really began, a decade ago, when I was toying with the idea of attempting another book. At the time, I had already written a dozen and had sickened a score of editors who had returned my pristine manuscripts along with polite and discouraging letters of rejection.

Back in those early years, my idol was Sloan Wilson, who had written *The Man in the Gray Flannel Suit.*

So I had tried, always failing, to be a second Wilson, writing about learned and sophisticated people, along with other minutiae about which I knew nothing.

Undaunted, and wearing my usual winning and optimistic grin, I waded into my story, about a family, a boy, and a pig on a Vermont farm. Its title, which I had not yet established, came when I wrote the final chapter: *A Day No Pigs Would Die.*

This novel, as you perhaps know, is our personal story. So, without thinking much about it, as I wrote, I gave the family in the book the name of Peck. I was the boy, Rob.

My editor at Knopf (a name, speaking of monikers, that no one can pronounce without a hairlip or an overbite) was dead set against my using my own name.

A battle ensued. *Fur flew!* It was a cold winter day in New York, so I was wearing my mink parka.

"It's *my* book!" I screamed at my editor, intent upon showing how much *character* my chief character now flaunted in manhood; even though, as I hollered, I knelt to kiss his ring.

Upshot: The book, willy-nilly, got published, won limited acclaim, and launched my authorship as all the Pecks stayed snugly tucked into my pages.

"Ah!" I said one day, cashing checks, tenderly hoisting each one up from the bin of my wheelbarrow. "Why not use myself again as a character?"

I did in my book of poems, *Bee Tree.*

Now flushed (and flush) with triumph, and having traded in my wheelbarrow for a pickup truck, since B.O. (barrel overflow) was becoming a problem, I decided to ride a free name to death.

(12)

Soup was born.

If you don't know who Soup is, and you never watch television, ask a kid. Soup Vinson was my boyhood pal. He was slightly more than a year older than I was—tougher, brighter, even more handsome, and the indisputed hero of (let me count) all six books in my *Soup* series.

But old Soup doesn't tell the stories. Rob does.

All the *Soup* books are written in the first person, strictly from little Rob's point of view. The readers see and hear Soup through only Rob's eyes and ears; a reader is never allowed to know what Soup is thinking, feeling, or scheming.

That was, in real life, the way we horsed around.

He started trouble. I took the rap. Rob Peck, in the books, is merely the fall-guy shadow, the drag rider behind the herd, a recording Boswell to a dominating Johnson, a Watson for Holmes, a Laurel for Hardy.

It's not great literature; but for kids, it works.

And it's so much fun to write a *Soup* book, because all I have to do is remember the joy, and agony, of being the richest boy on Earth . . . one who has a best pal.

How about *you?*

Was there, in your childhood, one very unique contemporary who was a degree more daring, more innovative, a real instigator of harmless mischief? Sure there was.

Hold it!

Right about now, an emerging writer can suddenly go astray and think that the book is about the other kid. No, it ain't. Your story must be about *you*—not about Soup, but about how Rob is affected by the friendship.

Soup is the mirror in which I admire myself in those carefree days of boyhood.

You, as a writer, are the only center of your childhood universe; pals, profs, and parents revolve around your awareness. Soup is not my only moon. For, like Saturn, other moons circle about my recollection:

Janice Riker, the school's moronic bully.

Miss Kelly, our revered teacher.

Eddy Tacker, a lout with lip.

Miss Boland, county nurse, a hippo of health.

Norma Jean Bissell, the peach-cheeked damsel for whom I ached like an impacted molar.

Mr. Jubert, lanky owner of the local candy store, hardly exists at all, *until* his establishment is invaded by two young customers, Soup and Rob, whom he cautiously eyes with well-founded mistrust.

You, my author, are your apple's core.

You're the camera, the god to cast your drama, making those around you merely the supporting players. Of all the members of the baseball team, only you stand on the pitcher's mound, toe the rubber, and spit on the ball.

Accomplish this by envisioning yourself as *the only one with eyes*.

Indeed, you are the balloon vendor, parading the carnival's midway . . . and up from your hand fan the strings that anchor spheres of air inside rubbery coats of many colors.

You stand as Joseph before his bowing brothers.

"Yup," you may say, "but Peck is not a character in *all* of his books."

Wrong. Although not by name, my personality (such as it is) seeps into most of my books. I know that I am Fawn in *Fawn*. And I'm Benet in *Eagle Fur*.

Hating to admit it, I am old Mr. Kirk in *Kirk's Law*.

So many novels, especially the *first* ones, by so many authors are autobiographical. Hardly ever, however, are they same-name stuff like *A Day No Pigs Would Die*.

To conclude, whether or not you use your own name for a character is unimportant. If you want to, do it. If not, coin a name. What *is* pivotal is this: Anchor at least one chief character into a definite personality, the one inside your soul.

The character you know best is *you*.

This is important. What *you* see, hear, and feel about other people you know well, or casually, is the raw material for an entire shelf of books. I know. I've published thirty-three of them.

(14)

Who is your hero?

You don't tell the story. *He* does. So, you should inquire: *Who* are the people who surround him? Whoa! Let's back up a step. Maybe you don't tell the story. Yet, please let me holler, *you* must become the hero who thinks, talks, acts, and feels . . . in the center of the crowd.

I am all my heroes.

Most times, I get away with it. Yet, on occasion, my editor's eye will pop and his pencil itch, when he detects an obvious Peckian pronouncement. I expect this. When this occurs, an editor is merely performing his job, and well.

These deletions, which willy-nilly always follow, don't always upset me. I'll fight to keep some of them in the story and even win a round or two.

Again, I repeat: It's easier for an editor to delete than it is for him to add or to suggest additions for you to make. Therefore, I am not in the least shy about Pecking up my people. I dump more Peck into my characters than water into Jell-O.

Why do I do this?

The answer is pig simple. Because I've got so much of *me* to give. Like you, I am abrim with likes, dislikes, talents, cumbersome inabilities, joys, triumphs, and failures . . . so why should I even consider wasting such a storehouse?

Okay, right about now you're possibly confessing that you don't really know yourself. Here's how to meet this wonderful hunk of humanity . . . *you:*

Start with five sheets of fresh paper and make five distinct and honest lists.

1. This is what I *like*.
2. This is what I *don't like*.
3. This is what I *want*.
4. This is what I *don't want*.
5. This is who I *am*.

Do them in that order. For this reason: If you do, then number five will come a lot quicker.

I did this exercise a long time ago. What's more, every once in awhile, I do it again. And again. Strange how my tastes change; yet the basic Vermont-bred Peck remains solidly constant. It isn't easy, or admirable, to cast aside what a boy learns at his mother's knee.

Please, once you fill your five pages, don't flash. Do not show them to anyone. Not everyone is as honest with himself, or herself, as you have just been; and your family and friends may even suspect you've gone bananas. You've been so *straight* that they'll suggest you wear a matching *jacket*.

Once you've met yourself, face to face, you will be armed with a ton of material that you can pour into the molds of your characters. Do not skimp.

Here's another trick:

Let's imagine that you have two characters in your story, and they are more or less the antithesis of one another. Pete is positive. Norton, negative.

So, as Pete likes a lot of stuff, trim his character with the tinsel and ornaments of your "this is what I like" page. Needless to say, Norton falls heir to page two, the list of things you don't like.

Helpful?

I do it. Why can't you? Void yourself into those characters of yours. Use yourself, and mix a ME into your menagerie. Besides, it's fun. You can slyly have a character say something, or tell somebody off on a page, in a manner that you or I wouldn't dare do at a cocktail party, at the office, or in church.

If you stray a bit or go full-out overboard, don't fret about it. Your editor will probably bring it back within the margins of moderation and taste. That's his job.

Your job is to sculpt the statue; his, to polish. So allow his blue pencil to etch away a wart. Please do not be too bashful to clutter your characters with your own personal characteristics. There's a lot of marble and granite in your own constitution that'll form one nifty statue. I use Peck.

You use *you*.

3
Character Building

Do your homework.

Writing is one heck of a rough racket, which means that if you dog it lazy, it will defeat you quicker than boo.

So, before you type *Chapter One* at the top of a virginal page (and then sit for weeks while you wonder what to do next) do your *homework* for each one of your characters.

Here's how:

John Xavier McCarthy, age 49.

Born in Boston in April of 1933. Son of Thomas Joseph McCarthy and the former Maureen O'Flynn.

John has one older sister, Kate, who broke her parents' hearts by marrying a Protestant. As a youth, John attended Roman Catholic schools, went one year to Boston College, then spent four years at West Point.

He decided to stay in the army as its rigidity, much like his authoritative early schooling, appealed to him, relieving him of too much thought, personal evaluation, or decision.

John got married. Babies came along frequently. He became furious when his wife told him that she was considering birth control.

He worked tirelessly for the election of Jack Kennedy to the U.S. Senate and, in 1960, hustled even harder to help elect him to the White House.

Soon after, John, as a first lieutenant, was ordered to Vietnam. Served well as an infantry platoon leader, was promoted to captain and company commander, then to major of a battalion. Finally advanced to rank of light colonel and appointed executive officer of a regiment.

Wounded once, received Purple Heart.

Saw continued infantry action and heavy casualties for almost five years. At last shipped back to USA, but he can't understand why his fellow Americans do not seem to welcome him home.

John sired seven children. Five sons. Two daughters.

None of his sons wanted to go to West Point. One of his daughters, Mary Agnes, got pregnant in college and had an abortion. Two of his sons currently live with their girlfriends, without marriage. Two other boys married; one now separated, the other is divorced. The fifth son, John suspects, is gay.

As time passes, John sees rapid changes in the Catholic church. The priest that John admires as a fine young man gets married. Nuns wear shorts, sandals, and sun dresses.

His disillusion intensifies as he begins to evaluate the Kennedys as bungling politicians who led America into a series of no-win disasters . . . Bay of Pigs, the Congo, and a decade of Vietnam. He gets drunk upon learning how Mary Jo Kopeckne died in the company of Teddy Kennedy.

Disgust complete, he shuns the Democratic party.

He resigns from the U.S. Army as only a bird colonel, though he was offered the star of a brigadier. Tries to fit into his wife's father's corporation.

Gradually he loses interest in business and in social activity. Knows his wife has romantic affairs yet doesn't care. He is almost an alcoholic. Alone, he writes sad Irish ballady poems, about love and war, and on how little his children will mourn for him when he dies.

All he believed in is dead.

Movies, TV, rock music . . . it all sickens him; he cannot accept how the tastes of his country, his family, his friends, have so eroded into shallow values, voiced by gutter language.

His head is rapidly balding. He's overweight. For the first time in his life he has money problems.

Attempts at selling real estate and insurance both fail. No gadget in his home seems to work anymore and no repairman seems to be able to do more than mail John exorbitant bills.

Financially desperate, he takes a job as a night watchman, under an assumed name. His days are spent in bed, rarely sleeping; yet he feigns sleep if any member of his family enters his bedroom. His wife has her own room.

He writes letters to Kate, his sister, but never receives a reply. Her telephone, two thousand miles away, is unlisted.

John no longer attends church.

His cigarette habits mounts to two packs a day, even more. Caught sleeping one midnight at the plant, he is fired from his job. No longer able to afford whiskey, he buys jugs of cheap wine, yet cannot sleep even though intoxicated.

To the man he has become, there is no present life. Only the past. Just memories of his father, mother, and sister, back in the days when everyone called him Jacky.

His wife no longer introduces him to any of the ladies who come to their home. Hearing them arrive to ring the doorbell, John dashes upstairs, to lock himself in his bedroom. In a pocket of his favorite gray sweater, he carries a rumpled photograph of Kate and himself when they were children.

There is a pony in the picture but John cannot recall the animal's name.

John's mouth is always dry, his face unshaven; and his hands tremble when, at early morning hours, he sneaks downstairs to try to fix himself food. Glasses and cups often fall to the kitchen tile floor, smashing, causing John to hide in a closet, panting in the darkness because he is now afraid of everyone, and of everything.

Trying to smoke, he sets fire to his sweater.

Finally, there is a car trip, to the country. His wife leads him into a strange building and tells him that he'll like it here. Around him are dozens of old men, and old women, all wearing shabby bathrobes. Some of them cry; others shout for no reason, yelling only to walls and bars.

"Where is Grace?" an old man asks him.

"I'm . . . Jacky," he answers. "I got a pony."

Finding a crayon on the floor of the Social Room, he prints MOM in large orange letters on the washroom wall. But they keep washing the word away. In a wild tantrum, he smashes the windows.

When he eats, he's allowed to use only a spoon.

What I've written is a character outline.

Please note that I rarely describe John Xavier McCarthy as a physical entity. Color of eyes and hair, height, and so forth, are not important. What matters is *the inner man*, the mind, the soul, and his vanishing values.

Notice how I surround him with tangibles, real things—a gray sweater, a photo of a long-ago sister with a pony. And a spoon.

Needless to say, when you outline a personal history, like that of John X. McCarthy, none of these notes goes into a manuscript. If, as you do it, dialogue comes to you, then zap it down. Let it flow. Yank the lanyard and boom it out. The notes exist for your use only. Now, once this homework is complete, you can begin *Chapter One* with your typewriter going at full clack.

Why?

Because you *know* your guy.

You hear him speak, feel his pain, and love him enough to reach out to touch the gray stubble of his face and say, "John, I'm right here with you." You'll begin to care, even to weep for this pathetic man whose life has fallen from the heights of West Point to one spoon, an old bathrobe, among other seniors whom he does not know and who shall never learn his worth.

Please permit Peck to urge you to outline blueprints, such as this, of people . . . until you create one individual who is so shiny, so sad, so irresistible and fascinating that you fall in love. And you want the world to hug him and hold him.

Who'll be pleased if you sweat out this homework?

You will.

Perhaps a chapter such as this one should have been entitled "How to Avoid Writer's Block" . . . which is staring at the empty page in your typewriter. My guess is that people who have this problem don't yet *know* their hero's character.

Character building is *outlining*.

So start with that blank sheet of paper and, instead of heading it Chapter One, outline *Character A*.

Answer these questions about him:

1. What's his name?
2. Where was he born and raised?
3. What is his religion and ethnicity?
4. Briefly (in order not to bog yourself down with cosmetics) what does he look like? Fat, thin, tall, short, muscular, flabby, gray, bald?
5. What does he believe in?
6. Where has he failed or triumphed?
7. Is he married, single, gay, divorced, or shy?
8. Most important of all, what kind of *work* does he do? And then, is he happy or discontented with it?
9. What are his hobbies? Sports? TV?
10. Is he neat or is he a slob? To establish this on paper, describe his dress, his closet, a drawer of his desk and the trunk of his car.
11. Can your mind picture him making something? Using a simple tool, perhaps, to shape the hull of a model clipper ship?
12. How do his *hands* behave? Relate them to tangible things that surround him.
13. Is he musical? Is there one special instrument that he

plays well or badly? Does he play it alone, for himself; or can he jam it up for an audience of friends or strangers?

14. What was his school and schooling like? Who was the teacher he respected and *why?*

15. What are the events, items, pets, pals . . . that he remembers for years?

16. Other than memories, what are the tangible trinkets he saves and treasures from his past?

17. Is he witty? If so, you cannot *tell* your reader that he is. Instead, you must let your dialogue *show* a reader exactly the witty remarks he makes.

18. How does he drive his car, tie his tie, gargle? Does he pick his nose, cough often, snore?

19. Read the editorial page of your newspaper and choose which opinions he agrees with or disputes. Does he argue bitterly, silently, or to anyone who has to listen?

20. What is his goal? Whom does he dream about, yearn for, hate?

Writing is work. And preparation.

But if you take the time to outline a character thoroughly, your writing will suddenly become far easier and much more fun. Your well-defined hero will *act*, *talk*, and *think* so rapidly that your typewriting fingers won't be able to keep pace.

Remember, when the question is, *What* am I going to write about? the answer is, *who?*

Build your character.

4
Author...
Butt Out

I've met hundreds of emerging writers.

Because I am Robert Newton Peck, an established author of more than thirty books as well as the original creator of the *Soup* and *Mr. Little* shows on the ABC television network, amateurs ask me to read their stuff.

I must be a masochist, because I do it.

Almost every emerging author I know commits this one cardinal boo-boo: Although not himself a character, he sneaks into his story, a place where he doesn't belong, to bore us to death with background.

Emerging writers want to butt in, interrupt their characters, who are masterfully *showing* me the story, and *tell* me the story themselves, as authors. This is unwise.

Writers, good ones, don't *tell* stories.

Characters *show* stories.

Yet the amateur writer is not content. He wants to take over the job. Here's how he manages to muck it up:

His hero, a little boy, is busily working in the cellar of his home, sawing and hammering out a birdhouse. As he works, his mother comes down the stairs.

All the kid sees is good old Ma.

But will the amateur writer let it go with that? No, not he. The amateur will then torment his readers by telling us that Mom is wearing a Bonwit Teller pinafore with off-the-shoulder puff sleeves, No Nonsense pantyhose, and sandals by Gucci.

Now, I ask you . . . what kid in his right mind, who's just whacked his own thumb with a tack hammer, is suddenly going to look up and see all that *Vogue* stuff?

He sees Mom.

Period. Maybe, just *maybe* she has a dish towel thrown over one shoulder and little Ricky knows that she's about ready to enlist his help upstairs at the kitchen sink. That's all he notices. He doesn't comment that her Mr. Kenneth hairdo is absolutely chic.

Following the Gucci and Bonwit Teller details, is the amateur author *now* willing to go on with the story about how Ricky's making a birdhouse for Mother's Day and not wanting Mom to see it?

No, there's more *author talk*.

This author klutz wants to tell us readers that Ma got born in Keokuk, was kidnapped by gypsies, and only years later escaped to become a meter maid in Galveston. He'll tell us her religion, her political and nocturnal preferences, her Social Security number . . . along with her age, weight, and blood pressure.

Hold it! He ain't through.

Birdhouse and Mother's Day now forgotten, he'll forge onward to tell us that she almost reached first womanhood at a drive-in movie on the stained backseat of Elmo McMurtree's 1951 Plymouth.

There was a double feature that evening, he'll inform us: *The Virgin Queen* and *Tonight's the Night*.

The author may even see, and tell us, Ma's remembering how Elmo had to take cold showers for at least a week. And of how little of either movie they managed to enjoy during four hours of uninterrupted tussle.

Halfway through the intermission that night, Elmo, cad that he was, claimed to her that he was no longer a boy but a man of genuine experience; and if she didn't believe it, she could ask Agnes Catlin.

Bit now in his teeth, our plebe author isn't about to whoa.

He might even go on to say how Agnes's garter became entangled around the gearshift stick which had been, due to faulty engineering in Detroit, inopportunely positioned.

Knowing little of Detroit, our author is indeed fortunate (even if his readers are far less so), because his Aunt Josephine lives near there and was able to supply him with vivid accounts about life on the gearshift shift of the Dearborn assembly line.

Design changes had finally come, we learn.

Those troublesome gearshift sticks had been, pardon the expression, retooled, and were now to adorn the steering wheel, where they would be out of harm's, and Elmo's, way. *Garterproof*, the new automotive brochures claimed.

Advertising ran with it from there.

TV screens all over America showed quick cuts of Plymouths, parked in the darker and more remote corner nooks of drive-in-movie lots, featuring only foot and ankle shots of Elmo and Agnes, busily ignoring Hollywood's most urgent release.

Often, the television commercials were beefed up with a few out-takes, discarded film footage of *Tonight's the Night*.

A voice-over announcer was also chosen, our amateur author says, on the strength that his Irish tenor was a dead ringer for Barry Fitzgerald's.

Ricky's mother had never met Mr. Fitzgerald. Yet, she had read the first chapter of *The Great Gatsby*.

In those early days of outdoor cinema, few Hollywood stars ever came round to the Keokuk area. She did, however, receive a full year's subscription to *Screen Secrets* for her sixteenth birthday, even though her advanced level of sophistication, plus a few more double features with Elmo, had thrust her socially way beyond its reading, not to mention pictorial, level.

After only the third copy had arrived, she switched her

subscription credit and from the same publisher received nine back issues of a magazine dedicated to intimate peeks of New York showgirls and their sporting ways, entitled *Broadway Bimbo.*

This became her favorite periodical, our author presses forward to inform his readers.

She spent many hours on the lap of her kindly old Uncle Dillon, who no longer had to hang around the local barbershop to thumb through rumpled copies that were often missing the spiciest photographs, due to the zeal of the more enthusiastic collectors.

Learning, via the grapevine, that Agnes Catlin was now flashing an engagement zircon, given to her by Elmo Mc-Murtree, the downhearted girl began to take long walks alone, and was eventually, as stated earlier, stolen by gypsies.

She got used to it, even though her gypsy captors never washed. Neither had Elmo.

Years later, now a meter maid in Galveston, she was writing out a ticket for an overparked, yet familiar, Plymouth. The car, as Fate would have it, turned out to be owned by a man who was also familiar.

Six months after the wedding, little Ricky was born. He quit school, however, at the age of five.

As he grew into boyhood, his only interest was in building birdhouses. He had constructed well over six hundred, so birdhouses hung by dozens upon scores in every cubic yard of every room. Worse yet, the little stinker left the windows open so birds could occupy them, which they did. Ergo, every floor in their home was knee-deep with scat.

It had ruined every pair of Agnes's Guccis, especially those with the open toes.

In a fit of rage, she whipped her dish towel, knocking this latest plywood offering to the cellar floor, and then stomped on it, smashing it to splinters.

"It's okay, Ma," said little Ricky. "I'll build you another."

Advice to writers: Stay out of your story.

Let the child who is building his first birdhouse tell it. He doesn't know about Elmo, or Detroit, and readers don't care. What readers do care about is a wonderful paint-stained boy who is making a crudely constructed gift for Mom that she'll cherish forever. That's all the story is. For readers, for a mother, or for a kid, it's everything that counts.

So, to be a professional author . . . butt out.

Please note that this butt-out chapter follows the one concerning how to build a character outline.

For good reason.

Because the stuff you write in an outline is only outline stuff. You don't start listing it in your book in order to bore your readers who want to learn *not* about Elmo's caddy behavior at the Keokuk Drive-In. They want to read about Ricky's building a birdhouse.

Again, allow me to stress that all the information and detail you wisely listed in outlining the past and personality of Ricky's ma does *not* have to be shoehorned into the book itself.

The info informs *you*, not the readers.

Outlines serve to keep a writer consistent when dealing with what a character says, thinks, and does. The outline cannot sneak into the story to disrupt the action about a birdhouse.

When I write, there are a lot of outline notes, facts, and quirks that I never get around to using. Nonetheless, the outline facts serve me as a guide to keep my character in character.

· What do I mean?

Just this: If dear Mom was born and raised in Keokuk, I can't allow her dialogue to sound as though she had been reared in a chic apartment on Manhattan's Park Avenue.

A writer is a racer.

He must sprint in a lane. Stay within the lines—or, if you prefer, the outlines. These lines of white chalk keep the runner (the writer) moving forward. They prevent our weaving away to describe the churlish behavior of Elmo and his backseat charm. If your reader wants to unlock those intimate secrets, let him consult the flaming pages in the diary of Agnes Catlin.

Adhere to your here-now action.

Fret not that you'll waste your time on the outline. You won't. Mom's wholesome Iowa (Keokuk) upbringing will blast out louder than a Klaxon on your pages. Her sterling farm-family background, plus the moral fiber that fought off Elmo's groping advances, will come shining through and rear its head as she's rearing her young Ricky.

Her character will be as consistent as a row of Iowa corn.

Now then, I do fully understand how anxiously you long to discover more about the loves of Agnes Catlin. Sorry. You won't be able to read it in this chapter or any other. To fill you in on that score (no pun intended) would be author talk. Agnes's ample posterior wouldn't fit a birdhouse.

This author will butt out.

5
Narrative Drag

Announcer: Friends . . . do you suffer from . . .
Sound Effect: Low organ note
Announcer: . . . Narrative Drag? If so, run down to your local bookstore for a speedy dose of Old Doc Peck's Ready Remedy.

* * *

What, you ask, is Narrative Drag?

It's an ailment very similar to the problem in the previous chapter that emerging writers *cause*. Like Typhoid Mary, who was never sick a day in her life, the amateur writer is not a victim but a carrier.

We who read the stuff are the bored victims.

The symptoms of Narrative Drag pop up when the hero is alone and emerging writers tart boring us with giant pararaphs of dull thought, thought, thought.

How do you avoid it?

Doctor Peck's remedy is a combination of ingredients. Three, to be exact. The hero, even when he's all by himself in the solitude of his lonely room, does three things.

He thinks, talks, acts.

As I pointed out in another chapter, "Socrates and a Wide Receiver," thinking alone is not enough. Not even if you're Socrates.

Thought needs a breather.

So does our poor reader, who is trying to wade through pages and pages of introspection. Worse yet, during such passages the amateur author is oft tempted to shoehorn in his own philosophies, ignoring his drowning hero. I've been guilty of this.

"Rob," said Frances Foster, my dear editor at Knopf whom I respect and adore, "you've tarnished one of your characters."

"Who?" I asked.

"It's the schoolteacher, Miss Burnout."

"Tarnished her?"

"Yes, a bit. In Chapter Seven, when she's alone in the solitude of her lonely room, her thinking doesn't seem to be in keeping with her personality."

"How?"

"She's too Pecky."

"Beg pardon?"

"She is espousing *your* pet peeves, not hers. You sort of left her and me. All she's doing is *thinking*. Break it up with action and let her say things aloud."

In a scarlet blaze of artistic temperament, I slammed the phone into its cradle. But a minute later I called Frances back to tell her she was right. Too much thought.

I reworked my seventh chapter.

Doing so, alone in the solitude of my lonely room, I knew full well that thinking, by itself, was not enough . . . even though all of my thoughts glitter with genius and groan under weighty profundity.

"Gx%ßz!" I swore at my Underwood.

Rising from the desk in my oaken study, I stood at full height, faultlessly attired in a tweed jacket (with rumpled slacks, no socks, and wearing mocs for picturesque disarray).

Looking into a mirror, I could see that my bronze, rugged,

yet sensitively sculptured face was furrowed by fret. I spoke.

"Mirror, mirror, on the wall,

Who's most gifted of us all?"

My reflection then smiled. "Only you, Robert."

Self-love, I was thinking, is hardly an admirable practice. But how could anyone, even a chap as modest as I, resist the infectious, farmboy, scarlet-lipped grin of Peck? It called to mind a classic cartoon:

A handsome Grecian couple wearing white togas, a boy and a girl, sit on a marble bench. The boy looks downward at the image of his face in a quiet pool of water. The girl, however, looks a bit apprehensive.

"Narcissus," she asks, "is there someone else?"

Tearing myself away from my mirror (an act that manifests my awesome powers of self-denial), I returned to my typewriter with one masterful stride.

"Underwood," I said, silently musing that such a name would have been perfect for the hero of my story, a termite, "I shall now bless thy keys with my immortal words." (I said all this aloud, in quotes, in order to prevent Narrative Drag.)

I typed.

The machine, now chattering dutifully, seemed, if I may once again coin an inspired phrase, to hang on my every word. Miss Burnout, formerly too Pecky, was reverting back to her scorched and wilted nature. And with action.

As my long artistic fingers graced the keys, I toiled on and on into the wee hours, golden words darting through the night like kitchen roaches. No aging boxer on TV could ever have hawked a spray so nimble as to overtake such furtivity.

"*Finito*," I sighed at last, happy that my mail-order French lessons were finally paying off.

The chapter about Miss Burnout's being alone in the solitude of her lonely room was now complete. My genius had calmed the troubled sea of her discontent. Her lover, a local principal who had formerly been the football coach, had climbed her ivy wall, gained her balcony, and entered her domain.

I felt a rub upon my leg.

"Yikes!" I yelled.

Could it be Drambuie, our cat? No, I knew it could not; a passing truck had flattened one of Drambuie's lives, rather appropriately, right after dinner.

Could it be my leggy secretary, Illicita, whom I thought had undulated home? Had she returned, climbed hand over hand up the ivy of my wall, gained my balcony, intent upon gaining my strength?

"Illicita," I whispered. "Is it *you*, my sweet?"

Alone, in the solitude of my lonely room, thoughts raged through my tormented mind. Illicita had come back to me. Once more our scarlet and seething lips would hanker, hunger, *have!* My body, a battery now charged with renewed voltage, was electric with anticipation. I smiled softly, remembering the amp-packed pet name that Illicita sometimes called me. Old Die Hard.

My hand fell to find another. *Hers!* Oh, how I yearned t'would be Illicita's. But no, t'was not to be. Looking under my desk, I saw not my leggy lass, but Muhammad Ali.

"Roaches," he said.

As I saw him spraying, I hoped he would spare at least a few of my golden words.

My head swam. No, I was hallucinating again. Neither Ali nor Illicita nor Drambuie was beneath my desk. I'd been working too hard. Alone, in the solitude of my lonely room, I'd been thinking and talking and acting. Level-besting to relieve Narrative Drag.

Thoughts blurred my troubled mind.

No man as robust as I could ever forget Illicita and our moments shared; she at her steno pad, I at my mirror. How I fondly recalled the pet name I had given her as she took dictation, Shortarm, a handle that seems so suited, so right.

Agonized, I raced around my lonely room, hurling furniture, mindless of the mayhem I was causing to the image of Grand Rapids.

"Ouch!" I yelled, barking my shin on my sleeping dog, whom I had given a pet name, Creme de Menthe, because he was green.

"Good dog," I said, stroking his silky ears, longing to apply a similar technique to Illicita. Tired at last, I sank to my cot, relieved that I had blended *thought, talk,* and *action* into the solitude of my lonely room.

I had conquered Narrative Drag. And, I hoped, Illicita would be next. But not today. My last words fell from my scarlet lips.

"I'll worry about that tomorrow."

* * *

Now then, enough about Illicita and me. What do you learn from this chapter? If nothing, then you will persist in boring your readers with endless paragraphs (even pages and entire chapters) on how your heroine is alone and downhearted. Don't worry if it bores your readers. It won't ever reach them. Because first you'll bore an editor so badly, *and so briefly,* your novel won't be published.

How do emerging writers fall into the trap called Narrative Drag? And when they do, how do they eventually escape? Better yet, how do we writers avoid N.D. in the first place?

One at a time, please.

We writers fall into the N.D. trap whenever we rip the camera out of the hero's head, demanding that *we*, not he, tell the story to a reader. As I speak in public rather often, to yawning audiences, I realize how little of interest we authors have to say.

So it follows, logically, that we shouldn't make readers yawn either. Or editors.

The easiest way to bore a reader or an editor is when you, the writer, isolate your character from tangibility. A character who thinks, even though he sometimes must, isn't as exciting as a character who talks, spits, chews, sneezes, sings, dances, fights, golfs, hunts, fishes, and makes love.

Narrative Drag is *an absence of things*.

It happens when there is no telephone, no fork, no gun, no football, and no candle-lit bedroom.

But bring in an object and you've won doggone near half the battle. Sooner or later, good fiction has to be tangible. If you're wise, it'll be sooner, not later.

The tangible object does not have to be of epic proportions. It doesn't have to be an atomic bomb or Hoover Dam or Egypt's biggest pyramid. In fact, the tangible object can sometimes be more dramatic if it is tiny, or cheap, or even free. A needle in a mother's fingers. An acorn in the hand of a child. A bug on a leaf.

In order to drive home this lesson, as I'd pound a silver stake into Dracula's heart, I will repeat its key words. Memorize them.

Narrative Drag is an absence of things.

Bring a thing into the scene and your audience moves an inch forward on their seats, to be close to the stage. Again, let me stress that *the thing* doesn't have to be a bomb so large that it will blow up the Pentagon.

Allow your hero, when alone and remembering his grandfather, to bend over and pick up an acorn. Let your reader see how his fingertip strokes the brown husk, or taps its creamy moon. *Then* write how the hero remembers dear old Gramps and how he (Gramps) found another acorn, one like it, decades ago. That's when you share the seedy wisdom of Grandfather with your reader. Not with thoughts alone. With the tangible.

A *thing!*

Let your stripper toss Tex a garter.

Show your old baseball pitcher (who needs a shave and chews plug tobacco) handing a beat-up baseball to a kid who'll never throw it away. Then, when the kid is alone, you (the author) will have that baseball handy. Even at night, when the child is supposed to be sleeping. Where's the ball now?

Under his pillow.

Reaching under the pillow, a small hand finds the ball in the dark, remembers Old Lefty; a sleepy smile forms.

That's when the kid thinks, frets, worries. But don't do it without that old baseball. If you do, before you ever get ·published, you'll N.D. a lot of us to death. So use that acorn, that garter, or a very old ball. If you don't, you and your readers will regret it.

You'll be a very old unpublished writer.

6
The
Beer Buddies

What's the best show on TV?

Obviously, the answer cannot be a television *program*, because so much of TV is a junkyard. The answer has to be . . . a commercial. A bunch of beer buddies.

Miller Lite beer, with creative brilliance of their advertising agency, McCann-Erickson, has managed to assemble a super family of *folks*. Are they trim, dashing, handsome men, all looking *with it* in designer jeans? Hardly.

Most of them are retired athletes, poolroom princes yelling gutterball lines, flaunting locker manners; several are dressed like walking CARE packages, faces mashed by cleat or spike.

Is their chatter drawing-room charming, urbane, as though written by Noel Coward? No. They're beer buddies, guys who log leisure with lager.

The dialogue usually sinks to a shouting match. One team, the Has-Beens, is merely hollering "Tastes great!" at their opponents, the Over-the-Hill-Mob, who yell back, "Less Filling!"

Not fancy.

But the "Lite Beer from Miller" 4-word message roars loud

and clear, so the financial fellows at Philip Morris are looking up, up, up, at the sales chart.

They're making life lousy for the competition and Bud is sadder but wiser.

Every tribe needs a chief.

Rodney Dangerfield, who deserves far more respect than he gets (none) from his suds-soaked sidekicks, is usually trying his troubled best to restore order. On camera, not even one cauliflower ear is listening. Yet we TV viewers twist up the volume knob in order not to miss even one of Rodney's ribby remarks.

Lite Beer knows its audience. Guys who dig sports, bowl, shoot pool, and love literature . . . mainly Mickey Spillane, another heavy who helps Lite left-hook a light-foot image that the brand name itself might imply.

What we TV viewers see is a tough gang of gorillas in which a lady would be out of place.

Ah, but among the broken noses nestles a nifty blonde, playing her role perfectly with a low I.Q. and high measurements, cute enough to make Christie Brinkley look like Maude.

Casting is complete.

The atmosphere is sex, suds, and sports. Jocks and jokes. Yet there's always a *plot*. The pressure, as luck would have it, always plummets on poor Rodney Dangerfield, who must lean on the pool table, chalk his trembling cue, and sink the winning ball.

Rodney, although playing himself superbly, is really not Rodney at all. He's you and he's me . . . the common man whose dream has come true, because he's allowed to banquet with the beasts of Virdon.

He is Daniel in a den of Detroit Lions.

Bart Starr is missing. Also absent from the scene is Roger Staubach. Probably because their fine features wouldn't fit. Faces in a Lite commercial have to look more Beery than Wallace.

Lite can't run quarterbacks for pitch-outs.

Defensive tackles are the meat of the message, and Lite

must wisely know what beer drinkers look like.

So, big Ben Davidson, a former tackle for the Oakland Raiders, passes a bowling ball to (who else?) Rodney, who now quivers worse than Robin Hood's original equipment. Ben's basso warns, "All we need is one pin, Rodney."

Bubba Smith and Deacon Jones are there, too. As is Marvelous Marv Thornberry to round out this picture of pals in paradise; and the swill tastes swell, swig after swig.

In beer talk, it's brilliant brew.

Video Storyboard Tests, an organization that measures the popularity of commercials by asking TV viewers for their choices, ranks the Lite all-stars as television's top. It is art, a contemporary Our Gang comedy that both entertains and sells its suds.

In the past, you have seen scores of TV commercials that I have personally composed, cast, shot, edited, and aired. Few were ever as good as Lite's and none was better.

As an aspiring writer, study these Lite spots in order to notice how the cast of characters is so masterfully seasoned with variety.

Rodney is a refreshing respite.

They all use their own names. You can't top a moniker like Bubba or Deacon or Marvelous Marv—or, for that matter, a contrived yet appropriate stage prop like Rodney Dangerfield.

It's a beauty of a brew, a blend of banter, bicker, and bar. It says *beer*.

Yet it's more than that. In my opinion, what makes the Lite Beer commercial so compelling to watch is this: *Something's going on*. Beyond the beery burping, some event is about to come down, usually on Rodney; and we viewers can't wait to see how he tumbles into the pit of the problem and crawls out.

The pressure builds.

A great ape takes a bite out of a billiard ball as though it were softer than a peach, and Rodney knows that whether he sinks the winning ball or allows his quaking cue to rip the green cloth, he's in for trouble from whichever side loses its loot.

Nevertheless, aside from subplot theatrics, the message booms in like the U.S. Cavalry to save Rodney's neck from his un-Sanforized collar.

Why, in a book about characterization, do I include a chapter about a TV spot?

Well, for one thing, if you want to become a writer, be willing to study anything that is the best in its class. I'm not touting Lite as the best beer. It's merely got the best commercial.

Most of all, the variety of its casting is faultless. It is a Superb Bowl of personalities, and no two of them are alike. Such orchestration deserves the attention, if not the respect, of anyone who is in the throes of casting a novel. Too many amateur writers jell their characters in a single mold. Only the names differ.

Close your eyes.

I want you, please, to picture an entire symphony orchestra on a stage. The musicians are playing Verdi. But suddenly someone in the audience yells, "Fire!" All the musicians, in panic, go insane. Each musician grabs his *chair* and scoots off the stage.

All you have left is one stage and a vast variety of instruments.

That is exactly what a novel is. (Or at least its most common form.) It is one stage and a variety of instruments, all of which look and sound different. As your teacher, I do not intend to yell "Fire!" at you. Yet, when it comes to the folks in your fiction, I'm going to yell "Variety!" at you and onto your stage until I'm blue in the makeup.

Vary your folks.

I do not mean only cosmetically (outer appearance) but also spiritually, morally, intellectually. Your cast is your orchestra. They don't, however, live in absolute harmony. They squabble. (Remember that last party you attended, where some know-it-all stood up on the piano to proclaim that Alexander Hamilton was the best president the USA ever had.)

People differ, argue, fight.

Some yell "Less filling!" Others, "Tastes great!"

When the entire cast of your novel plays in total harmony, you may have a peachy orchestra but a pit of a story. So close your eyes again please. Now that all fifty musicians have left, let's imagine that fifty untalented members of the audience run up onto the stage, grab the instruments, and start to pound, strum, blow, and bow.

Now . . . that's a novel I'll read.

So, if you can, observe a Lite Beer commercial on your TV tube. You won't hear much of a symphony, but it's one nifty variety show.

It is a Lite Brigade to instruct any author who is scholarly enough to laud the art of casting, the craft of dialogue, and the simplicity of an innovative idea that appeals to folks, like all of us, who can appreciate fantastic fiction.

Watch, learn, and thank Rodney.

7
Milking a Scene

Gypsy Rose Lee was a stripper.

Her feathery and bubbly stage was her scene, her turf; and she never would have become a big-name ecdysiast had she shed her threads and shared her endowments in one beat of the tom-tom.

She disrobed slowly, very slowly, causing the fellows' Farenheit to rise merely by sliding one finger from a satiny glove.

Another genius was Charlie Chaplin.

In one of his many slient flickers, this creative comedian was caught in the company of some other guy's girlfriend. The other guy was twice the size of Charlie and, at once, challenged him to fisticuffs. To impress the fair lady, Chaplin accepted.

Do you think Charlie Chaplin threw a punch right away? Of course not.

Noticing that the big guy had taken off his coat and already had his dukes up, Charlie slowly removed his own coat. With nonchalance, he looked around for a coat hanger, finally finding one. Even though it was a black-and-white film, the audience could envision the big fellow's face redden with impatience.

Once the coat hung from a hanger, Charlie straightened both its sleeves, smoothed a lapel, and turned the side pockets inside out to brush away lint. Next, of course, Charlie had to roll up his sleeves. He managed not to roll them evenly and had to start over.

The action took place in a room.

To make space in which to fight, Charlie then decided to re-arrange the furniture, to straighten a tilted picture, and then to roll up the rug. He couldn't quite decide where to put the vase.

The audience didn't want to see a fight. What hypnotized us was Charlie's deftness at postponing it. Preparation made Big Guy madder than H. Yet, no sooner was one preparatory problem solved than Charlie adeptly would debut another.

No words exchanged.

Dialogue would have been excess baggage in a scene of such professional pantomime.

We usually liken *suspense* with drama, or melodrama—some murder mystery in which the audience knows that Dirty Dirk, armed with an ice pick, is hiding in the refrigerator, unbeknownst to dear elderly Aunt Allspice, who is now entering the kitchen.

Auntie stands with her defenseless back to the refrigerator door, which slowly opens, so we can see the silvery shine of the ice pick, an evil hand, an arm that raises and is about to strike.

Luckily, that's about the time Aunt Allspice hears (as we do) the buzzer, warning that her soft-boiled egg is ready, and away from the refrigerator she skips. Yet only to momentary safety.

Meanwhile, inside the Westinghouse and its store-more door, the climate is becoming a tad cooler than comfy. To make matters worse, Dirk is naked. He's been carrying on a feckless romance with Auntie's niece, Opal, who is also unclad inside the refrigerator, now complaining about the cold, and claiming that the whole sordid affair will make her frigid.

My, how I do get involved with folks.

Exciting fiction is folks *about* to do something. It's as much preparation as the act itself. We don't have too hairy a story if Dirk succeeds in giving Aunt Allspice a jolly jab in the jugular on his very first try.

I want you to read *Casey at the Bat*.

It's a poem, now long of tooth, which masterfully milks a scene of a mighty man of Mudville, a baseball player, who, with the bases loaded, can win the game by hammering a homer.

Like all classics, the poem is plain, simple; yet it is universal, examining the shortcoming of arrogance in a shortstop's terms.

Okay, you're saying. That baseball business is all well and good, but you want to know what's happening back inside the Westinghouse. What are those three kitchen folks doing? You want to learn if the refrigerator door is still open a crack (not wide enough, of course, for the little light to go on). Taste doth forbid.

Well, you win.

Auntie Allspice is sitting at her kitchen table, forking down an egg with one hand and, with the other, holding her latest copy of the *National Enquirer*.

Eating and reading, her back is to the icebox. Fortunately for Dirk and Opal, it's a tiny kitchen. Actually, more of a kitchenette. The crack of the door now widens. Again we see an ice pick held in fingers now blue with cold. We catch a glimpse of Dirk's evil face; and Opal, as she's rubbing her slowly-turning-to-purple veins and wondering if there's such a thing as a Supphose body stocking.

Somewhere in the kitchen, a canary chirps just as Dirty Dirk is about to do his dirty work.

Up jumps Aunt Allspice, escaping once again, now lovingly lining the bottom of Tweetie's birdcage with the *National Enquirer*. She adds extra birdseed and water because she is planning to go away for a long weekend in Phoenix to visit her beau, a retired art teacher named Sagebrush.

Observing that the refrigerator door is ajar, wider now,

and the little light inside is on, Aunt Allspice bangs it closed with a suggestive little bump and grind of one generously sized hip. Gypsy Rose Lee had always been her girlhood idol.

Inside, good old Dirk and Opal are plunged into total darkness. They're *locked in!*

But the weekend passes quickly since they have each other, along with a pleasing variety of drinks, snacks, and locked-in goodness that Opal can so delightfully serve, garnished with a sprig of parsley.

My guess is that it's impossible to instruct would-be writers how to milk a scene.

Your only hope is to try it yourself, as I did for decades, until you're rather good at it. But allow Peck to give you a hint. Do not let events happen too abruptly. Events in our real lives hardly ever do. Darken your sky; let us hear a rumble of distant thunder (or, if your story is set in New Orleans, a ramble of muskrats). Delay the lightning.

Amateurs always begin sentences with *Suddenly* . . .

Life doesn't happen that way. Neither does love. It unfolds, gradually, like a hideaway bed. A professional writer doesn't open a love scene with an orgasm. Love awakens slowly, with a shy smile, a wink, a timid touch. Drama does, too. In other words, as the helpless maiden is roped to the railroad tracks, we do not yet see the train. We only hear a distant whistle.

Milking a scene is one of many ways to show a character's personality to a reader.

Earlier in this chapter, we talked about how Charlie Chaplin used delaying tactics to avoid getting his nose punched to pudding. Which leads me to a hasty conclusion about something horrible that new authors tend to do.

They punch noses too quickly.

Wouldn't you, if you were reading a war novel, want to get to *know* the soldier before you fix his bayonet and send him over the top and into the teeth of gunfire?

Let's put it more specifically. I will now tell you that a guy in my outfit was killed overseas, in 1945. Well, are ya moved?

No, of course not. His name was Charles Dixon, born on a Nebraska farm, had freckles, didn't yet shave, and he played the harmonica, softer than taps, at night before we slept. We mailed his harmonica back to his folks.

No, you're not moved yet. But we're a whole lot closer to three things. One, to Charlie's death. Two, to my reaction to it. Three, to a reader's reaction.

As I write this chapter, I'm tempted (only tempted, as I won't do it) to amend its title to 'Milking a Novel.'

Why?

Because the reader has to get to *know* your characters, watch them laugh and struggle, before the twister hits the farm. Characterization, in fiction, is a slow and gradual exposure. You, the writer, strip and chip away the Halloween costume a thread at a time. Show me, please, a broken knuckle beneath a wedding ring before you abruptly rip away the face mask.

Let me see a foot tap to a tune of fiddle music at a barn dance.

Before you show me (your reader) your character being shot, at least show him being vaccinated Show me how he eats, ties his tie, or gargles.

With the magic of time-lapse motion picture photography, we can, in only a few seconds, watch a bud open to become a blossom. On a screen, yes. Not in a book. Mother Nature doesn't grab a bud and wrench it into a rose. She unfolds it oh so slowly.

So do writers.

Sure, we readers want to see and touch and inhale your little rose. Yet let us, please, first view its bud. Its seedling. Or even its gardener. Does its bush struggle upward to survive a late April snow? Show me an early leaf. June may be pink with petals, but April is green.

Do not deny me the gradual greening of your character. Before you show me a dead soldier's body, show me one of his childhood toys.

Perhaps one little lead soldier.

Corny? Of course. As I have written before, so much of life that is worth holding and cherishing forever is corn. My father once said that what made Vermont a good place to live was the fact that we knew how to turn grass into milk and corn into hogs.

Never shy away from corn.

Readers, not a manjack of us is nearly as cynical or as sophisticated as he claims. Oh, perhaps in bravado, in front of others. But alone, *when we read*, our social dukes are down and a yellow buttercup can tickle our chins.

I once was a soldier. Know this: Men at war are not chest-thumping gorillas. They sing "Back Home Again in Indiana" and weep. Not often do they smirk when they observe harlots feeding hungry and homeless children. When the C Company cat is killed, they bury her with reverence and prayer.

Philosophers claim that war brings out the worst in us. Perhaps so. Yet I saw it also bring out the best in us. Either way, it brought out the *all* in us.

Corn?

You betcha. Because when the corn quits being either grown or written or read, the human spirit will turn brown on its stalk.

Your book is your scene.

Milk it. Break bread before breaking bodies. Do it with sweetness and gentleness, the same way you once milked a cow, or gave milk to a child.

Milking, in a sense, is what characterization is all about. It is the sweet bud of professional authorship. Needless to say, your novel can't be all milk and honey or milk and corn. Eventually, your soldier's hours of horror will come, to spur a reader to wonder if ever he will again plow his Indiana.

"Enough of this," you bellow. "What about Dirk and Opal back at Aunt Allspice's kitchenette? Did they survive a wanton weekend in a refrigerator or did their ardor cool?" You deserve an answer. I'll write one, knowing full well that amateurs begin sentences with "Suddenly."

A burglar broke in while Auntie was away. Dirk, exhausted from romantic exertion, was fast asleep in the vegetable drawer. But not Opal. She heard the heavy male footsteps just outside the refrigerator door. Then, the click of its latch.

Suddenly, she froze.

8
Operation Sex Change

Hold on.

This chapter isn't what you think it is. Or hope it is. It's only about how I, a male, write from a female point of view.

My being a girl started with *Trig*.

Soup was promising to be continuous in print and on TV. I'm now working on the seventh book of that series, which is about two boys. So, I hunched, a series for girls might fly.

Elizabeth Trigman is a little girl, tough and tender, who isn't going to be pushed around by two males, Bud and Skip. Her gimmick is a toy she owns, a very large one, a genuine Melvin Purvis Junior G-Man machine gun that hoots like a howitzer.

The series is told entirely from Trig's point of view.

I am a man of 55, but it's my job as an author to sort of become a little girl like Trig, live inside her head, looking at life through her glasses, which are usually foggy or smeared with dirt.

To become a complete writer you have to learn to be everybody, every character in your book. This is difficult—especially when it comes to seeing with the other half's eyes. Like all men, I don't understand women at all.

I'm too simple and they are too complicated.

ERA, to me, seems to hang on like a legislative Karen Quinlan, dying, not yet dead. I can't ask any young girl to be drafted or to fight to save me. It makes more sense for *me* to go to war, even at my age, rather than plunking her into a foxhole.

I've had my life and I want her to live hers.

I used to think of women as people like my mother, who never, in her entire life, held a job. But today's mom is apt to be divorced, receiving little or no financial help from the jerk she foolishly married, and working to support a child. My observations thus tell me that many American males are weaklings.

What holds a family together these days? Alimony.

It's just plain rotten that when a woman today works a man's job, she can't earn a man's wage.

Many of the property laws in a good many states stupidly favor a husband and insult female dignity as well as female intelligence. We have only to look at Congress and their repeated budget deficits to realize the limited mind of man.

Prior to becoming a novelist, I worked for decades in New York City. I wrote TV commercials. Hating now to admit it, I cast housewives standing at washing machines, telling America, "My whites are whiter, colors brighter."

In my commercials, the deepest problem in Sue's life was fighting wax buildup or static cling.

You've come a long way, baby.

Today's American male, in too many cases, has degenerated into a simp whose concern is his hair blower instead of feeding his mate and offspring. The American female, in the meantime, has bloomed with a new strength I find admirable.

I fervently pray that women rise, prosper, and soon make up *half* of our Congress and our courts. Our government's a mess because we males have botched it.

Respect for today's woman, however, is too often just words and no action.

Some of the most frail men I know say *chairperson,* and I hope most of them fall into a *person* hole.

If the women's movement is to succeed, here's one old man's advice to women. If you pick a male to bugle your cause, pick a John Wayne. Not an Alan Alda.

Also, please choose more charming female leaders to represent you.

It's my hunch that few of us, regardless of gender, want our daughters to grow up to look like Betty Friedan or Bella Abzug, or to sound like them. It boils down to this: Most of us don't prefer to live in a strident atmosphere of roaring macho or trumpeting feminists.

I want ladies and gentlemen.

So do you.

Ergo, if you're a male writer, write about the kind of women you'd like to have for friends or neighbors. Write about the little girl you would cherish for a daughter. Gentle and guts aplenty.

Try a book I wrote called *Last Sunday.*

It's told from the point of view of a little girl named Ruth Babson. As her name is Ruth, and she's a whiz at baseball, the kids call her Babe and she digs it. Her mother does not; she is no baseball fan. Neither is Babe's father.

But there *is* an adult fan in the family . . . a maiden aunt who comes to visit, Aunt Hobart, who knows baseball—more, who sees her scruffy little niece as the child she never had. And perhaps as the homer she never hit.

Beauty is variety.

So *vary* your female characters as much as you vary your males. For years, Hollywood (and my TV spots, which now shame me) pictured the female merely as Helpless Harriet. She always had to fall down when she and the hero were escaping. Her role was pretty, dull, and totally unrealistic.

The hardest book I ever attempted to write was *Clunie.* It's about a retarded girl. The story, however, is told not only from Clunie Finn's point of view, but also from the minds of several characters. One of them is Sally Rowe, beautiful, wealthy, and somewhat spoiled. She is all that Clunie is not.

Sally cannot understand why the hero, Braddy Macon, a boy she finds interesting, wants to walk Clunie home so that some cruel children will not torment her.

As for Clunie, I had to force myself to become a retarded teenage girl who is chubby, wears big shoes that she resents, and yet knows that she is different.

Even so, Clunie wants to look like Sally.

As I wrote, I wanted to be that tortured soul inside Clunie Finn, loving her strange and frightened father, adoring animals and daisies, aching to have one friend. Just one. Clunie wonders why her father frowns when he sees her coming home with Braddy, the innocent boy who has been so sweet to her.

To add to my problem, I had to be more than just clunky Clunie the teenager.

Her characterization demanded that I become Clunie the mental tot. To me, her mind had to be a citadel of early childhood. Simple joys and fears.

To balance her weak brain, I gave Clunie a powerful body. For years, she and her father had worked the farm. She'd hauled, hefted, and tugged herself into almost an ox of a girl.

Clunie loves Teacher, a woman at school whom the reader never really meets, except through Clunie's appreciative and adoring thoughts.

Thus, I began to think of myself as Clunie Finn, an odd combo of physical might and mental retardation, in a high school society where boys and girls are perhaps too rapidly straining to be men and women.

It is baseball season, spring, and young juices are surging, the kids aching to prove themselves. Inside my gentle Clunie, womanhood softly begins to bud. Feelings she cannot comprehend. A healthy body now battles a childish mind that could be, perhaps, too limited to discipline desire.

Clunie's personality sharpens through the use of two young male characters:

1. Braddy, who is kind and protective.
2. Leo Bannon, who cannot have Sally Rowe, and whose body and mind are screaming to prove his manhood to himself. Clunie becomes a target to be teased; then, to be taken.

Clunie, although she cannot bear to harm any person or any animal, not even a daisy, is aware that Leo, though smiling, is fixing to do her harm. Leo's cold smile is not like Braddy's warming grin.

If you read *Clunie*, you'll see.

It was a difficult book to write because I had to attempt to be not only a female but also a retarded teenage girl. I took several trips to a home for retarded children and observed them, day after day, as they tried to work or play or feed themselves.

One particular young lady looked at me and smiled a chubby smile. Her shoe was untied. So I approached her very slowly, quietly, and then did a strange thing. Bending down, I untied my own shoe. I let her watch me as I retied it. Then I retied hers.

That's all it took. She followed me everywhere I went as my shadow. And cried when I, out of necessity, went to the men's room.

One day I brought a camera and took her picture.

What she liked best was when I played the home's beat-up piano. As I played, she sang. Not in words. Only noises. But whenever I'd stop playing to listen to her, she would stop. Then we would both laugh at each other. It became a game. It was one of the few areas in which this pathetic and wonderful girl manifested any intelligence.

She talked but made no sense.

I liked her, even though it would be hard to explain exactly why. It was somehow more than pity. Perhaps we all tend to warm to people who like us. She liked me. It was truly an honor, like when I won the Mark Twain Award. It was a genuine thrill.

I won't tell you her name because it's sort of a personal secret. Besides, as it was a very unusual name, like Clunie, my flashing it on a printed page could embarrass her parents.

At night, after coming home from visiting her, I would lie awake and pretend that I was a retarded girl who had a very tall friend named Rob who played a piano for me.

I did one other thing.

Wearing a pair of heavy ski mittens, I tried to dress myself, eat, and play the piano. Not in front of her. These acts I performed in my own home, when alone. Our maid, who caught me at it, probably thought I was nuts. She was correct. Because, mittens and all, I was actually acting retarded.

The female part was hardest. I tried wearing a long wig and brushed my false hair. It didn't help much.

What helped was giving that special child a hug, a song, and a laugh. Merely allowing her simple and female thoughts to touch me as though I were not her special gentleman caller, but rather her sister, who cared. I decided that what I really wanted, and finally discovered, was the little girl inside me who wanted to please another child.

To conclude, I believe that all humans are, inside, half male and half female. You are a product of a mother and a father, so it makes sense. God's plan.

If you are a big strapper of a man, and you deeply love a woman, you can perhaps best show your love by being, in quiet and private moments, the *sister* that she always wished she had.

Therefore, it is not surprising that both male and female characters, and characteristics, lie dormant inside you, waiting to be released upon your pages. This is my philosophy on the matter; and if you disagree, beware.

I'll hit you with my purse.

9

How Characters Multiply

As you read this book, one pointed postulate is repeatedly being jackhammered into you:

FICTION IS FOLKS. A novel's key element is characterization.

So, you may ask, how do you do it? How do you spawn characters? Whence do they hail? Does a doctor bring them in a black bag? Or a stork?

Here is one simple way to create characters. It is not the only method, but is one that works for Rob Peck, book after book. Start with an *issue*.

Let's pick a real zinger, one that's bound to rub you, me, and every cat in town, the wrong way.

We'll write a novel about abortion. This is our issue. So we'll look at a specific *situation*, a typical one, evolving from the issue.

As good professional writing is merely common sense, this question naturally pops up. *Who* would be the center of an abortion novel?

1. a Royal Canadian Mountie?
2. a monk from Tibet?
3. a matador swording bulls in Madrid?
4. a Watusi warrior?
5. a young girl, age 16, in high school?

Obviously, as we eliminate the absurd, we can see how only one of the above personalities is natural for our story.

We have, therefore, teenage Sally in trouble.

Also we have Tom, her boyfriend. Add to this the fact that both Sally and Tom have parents, and we're already up to six folks.

Is there one special *teacher* at the high school whom Sally admires, respects, and trusts? Would she tell her problem to Miss Hodge? Or is there a very understanding *minister* or *priest* at the church Sally attends?

Finally, is there a *doctor?*

Yes, there has to be. But the personalities of doctors vary as much as humanity allows, so we must now nail down the eccentricities of his nature.

Is our Dr. Brown old or young?

Quite possibly Dr. Brown is a man who is personally opposed to abortion. On the other hand, he plays golf with Sally's dad. Perhaps, years ago, it was Brown who delivered Sally at birth. Is he willing to perform an abortion in a town where there exists a century-old ordinance against such an operation?

Sally delays, hoping her problem will go away. Then she finally goes to consult Dr. Brown.

Now, if Brown refuses to abort Sally's problem, there is another doctor who lives in a shabby section of town and perhaps no longer practices medicine legally. Is this man some unwashed drunken butcher plying his trade in the back room of a garage at night?

Sally's mother is perhaps more innocent, by the standards of today, than is her daughter. It is almost impossible for her to face the issue that Sally is pregnant. For some strange reason, the pregnancy eludes the mother's thoughts. Her mind is preoccupied with the horror of knowing that Sally is not married and yet was making love.

Sally Murphy has told her mother that she is pregnant. But not her father. Sam Murphy is a decent man with one devil of a temper. Upstairs, he keeps a loaded pistol in the drawer of a nightstand beside his bed. Sally has observed that her father has always acted rather coolly toward Tom, especially whenever the youth arrives on a motorcycle.

Tom Rowley has been bombarded by sex . . . movies, television, the lyrics of today's music.

His older brother, Hank, told him that he won't be a man until he makes it with a girl. In fact, Hank lied to Tom, telling the younger brother that he, Hank, has made it with lots of girls. Hank has voiced such claims even though he had never, not even once, "scored."

Hank's resentment of his younger brother's triumph, if the act can be so called, builds a jealousy that is coupled with his own sexual frustration.

Tom doesn't want to quit high school, get married, and plunge himself into the pit of early debt from which he will possibly never escape. He wants to go to college and become an engineer.

Sally is confused, not knowing what she wants.

Only a few weeks ago, all she wanted was Tom Rowley. Her one desire was to have everyone in the school think of her as Tom's girl. Last year, Tom had hung around with Sue Wiggin, one of the cheerleaders, a girl whom Sally dislikes and envies.

During the very moment when Sally and Tom made love for the first time, Sally was not thinking completely of Tom. Her thoughts were of Sue Wiggin, and how angry she would be if she could only see the two of them totally united.

How understanding is the minister?

It's possible that he has forgotten that he and his wife *had* to get married. In his study and with Sally in tears, he reads the

Bible to her and tells her that God has punished her for being so rife with sin.

Reverend Alston's wife overhears.

As soon as this happens, we have yet another character to pour into the pot.

Mrs. Alston knows exactly the fear Sally Murphy, age 16, is enduring. She is aware that Sally is troubled by the thought of terminating a fetus, a life, in order to save her reputation.

She sees Sally not as a sinner, but as a very frightened child, a girl who did the wrong thing for a wrong reason. Mrs. Alston knows that Sally, a sophomore, is even less prepared for motherhood than she is for next week's geometry quiz.

Tom refuses to go to school.

He cannot bring himself to go to Sally's home or even to telephone. Nor can he suffer the resentment of his older brother, who seems to hate him ever since the night he told Hank that he and Sally had made love.

Tom Rowley, in a panic, runs away.

He has an uncle who lives fifty miles distant, Uncle Ralph, his mother's younger brother. Ralph is a bachelor who lives alone. He is only ten years older than his nephew, yet, for his youth, surprisingly mature. He offers a patient ear and an understanding heart, telling Tom that the measure of manhood is not sexual. It is responsible.

Ralph has a girl, Tillie.

She becomes fond of Tom because he, in a youthful way, reminds her of Ralph.

Two years ago, Tillie had an illegal abortion. This is a secret that she shares with Tom, even though she never has shared it with Ralph. A doctor told Tillie that she cannot become a mother.

To sum it all up, because of an *issue*, we now have a variety of characters involved. Some show reason; others, temper. Some are devoted to helping Sally and Tom; others are concerned with their own hurt, family reputation, and social condemnation.

As well as principals, we have town folks, all self-ordained experts on abortion . . . convinced how right they are and how wrong everyone else is.

How did I do this? What method did I use, what steps, to create so suddenly a complete cast of characters?

I started with one person.

Sally Murphy.

This is logical. Because, seeing as our issue is abortion, we must select a prototypical situation. Who would be at the hub of such a wheel of potential spokes of character? A pregnant girl.

One of the secrets of successful fiction is knowing where to begin and how.

You *don't* roll a fresh white sheet of paper into your Underwood, type *Chapter One* at the top, and then stare blankly at it for a year. You *do* begin with an issue. Which requires a character. In this case, Sally Murphy.

Then you jot down her age, where she lives, her economic level, her I.Q.—plus every helpful fact that you can create to outline Sally's personality and environs. This is exactly what I do, time after time, for each novel I write. I do it for one pig-simple reason.

It works.

For my dough, the books that are the easiest to write are those that have one central character. A *hub*. And from the hub, this principal porcupine will sprout the quills of all, or most, of the other characters.

Problem:

Where is the camera? Is the story told entirely through Sally's eyes, from her young and frightened and confused point of view? Offhand, I would quickly answer *yes*. But this is no ironclad rule.

Perhaps the story of Sally's pregnancy is told by her younger sister. It could be. But I'd need some strong convincing from my own logic, and from my editors, before approaching it in this manner. Because I believe that the situation of carrying a child, at Sally's age, is so highly personal, we readers would want to be inside Sally throughout.

Still and all, always consider point of view (who tells the story?) before you begin. *And* be openly willing to change it, once you decide your camera angle could be stronger if moved to another location.

To conclude, issues are nifty things to write about. They spawn situations. A situation can birth a litter of characters. Multiplication of characters does not depend on two parents. One is plenty.

One little hub, one Sally.

I cannot predict how your novel about Sally Murphy will end. Nor can you. Only your characters, each a mix of strength and weakness, can determine the finale.

As I write this chapter, it is difficult to rip away from Sally, an imaginary character, as her situation is so tragic.

All I know is that I want also to introduce a character, a strong one, who plays the total realist. A person who will say that *if* abortions take place (and perhaps they always will), let them please be performed in a hospital with modern equipment by competent and caring professionals.

Not by an unwashed drunk in a dirty garage.

10
Tools
in Hand

I urge you to watch Billy Graham.

Years ago, in New York, it was my good fortune to meet him personally. He has eyes that would melt granite; plus an athlete's frame, one that appeared lithe, rugged, resolute.

As he offered me his hand, with no hesitation, I was welcomed by a grip that would make the village blacksmith feel like Little Bo Beep.

A hard hand.

Yet the smile on his face was soft, Christian, making me feel that his heart had room for one more friend. I don't guess it's necessary to add that young Robert Newton Peck was quite impressed.

A few evenings prior, I had gone, as had countless thousands of others, to the old Madison Square Garden.

It was free. We common people were there, twenty thousand of us, modestly dressed as average folks are. Somehow, this giant indoor arena that reeked of boxing sweat, horse shows, and elephant dung from a recent circus became a quiet country chapel.

Onstage, one thousand voices rose from a rafter-ringing choir. Ethel Waters, a black lady with a silver voice, sat in the choir's front row like the dignified duchess she is. Her gray hair was a halo.

George Beverly Shea, the gospel singer, boomed out his baritone to give us "Roll Jordan Roll."

At the time, I was a young cynic.

I had come to see some sawdust clown jump through an evangelical hoop. My face was itching to smirk. My soul wanted to disbelieve rather than devote.

Billy Graham began to preach.

I'd already seen Hank Aaron hit a baseball and heard Van Cliburn hit a piano, so I knew what *super* was.

As I write this chapter, decades have passed; yet what my eyes still see is how Billy Graham held his Bible. It was the tool of his trade and he handled it with a confident ease.

He was John Wayne coiling a lasso.

Allow me to urge you, as an emerging writer, to consider giving a proper *tool* to a character. Let your Captain Ahab hold a harpoon, finger the barb of its point, and balance its shaft.

Is this some author's cheap trick? Not at all. Quite to the contrary, it is genuine literary leather.

Let your readers see your fisherman pinch a grub to a hook, or quietly mend his seine. Moments like this blossom characters. Folks of fiction come alive in this manner . . . doing their *work*.

Strong men perform tender tasks.

In fact, it is only strong men who master the value of tenderness. The sissy is loud and rude, unsure in his vanity, unproven among his fellows and the ladies.

The rabbit softness of men I have known . . . lumberjacks, football tackles, butchers of hogs, farmers and fur trappers and papermill crews . . . each has been a teacher tender.

To show this, use tools.

Warning:

There is a distinct difference between a tool and a weapon.

An ax builds; a tomahawk destroys.

Sometimes, even the tools of argument can become overly zealous. When the parties who oppose each other over a sensitive social issue turn emotional, each convinced he's totally right and the other folks totally wrong, the tool of the decent person can become the weapon of the maniac.

Moving on to a more pleasant subject, I ask you to read my novel, *Kirk's Law*.

In this book, a very old man, Sabbath Kirk, who resides in a shack in the Vermont wilderness, teaches a city boy how two men work one lumber saw.

Note also, please, his name. It's a soft name. Sabbath Kirk means Sunday Church. Yet my old gentleman is gruff, tacit, hard as a Yankee winter. Harder, for he has survived his share of winters—seventy of them.

His dog is as hard. Her name is Tool, oddly enough for this chapter. Tool's ribs show—leaner, meaner than hunger.

Your fireman, Jack, is exhausted, gritty, near frozen from ice water, scorched with flame, hurting from a fallen rafter . . . yet before his bath and rest, he flattens water from a hose, then refolds that hose with dedication into the rack at the rear of his giant red engine.

Jack's lungs still fight the fire.

His hands are purple, stiff, numb with cold; but he tends the tools before tending to himself. No talk is needed. Your reader sees Jack Germanski and knows him. And more, begins to care about his danger, his future, and his family.

A little girl is ready for morning school. At the door of their kitchen, her mother kneels, her hands busy with scissors, to snip off a raveling from a lace collar, one that she herself crocheted.

The scissors click. This noise says, "I love you, my child," more dearly than words.

Tools are not limited to drama.

They can also be comic. If you doubt this, you have only to close your eyes and envision the Three Stooges, or the Marx Brothers, wallpapering.

Repairmen are born comics. Your friendly plumber, Stilson Clogg, is never happier than when he ducks beneath your sink, where he can clang, bang, and swear. A pipe organ of sound.

Does he forget first to turn off the master water valve? Of course he does. Stilson's a master at making a mess. You may not be staggered by his craftsmanship, but you will be by his bill.

The world may stop in awe; yet when your John is backing up, Stilson plunges on. His fans (the Roto Rooters) are few, yet his tools number many.

Use them.

Characterization, please allow me to repeat, *is physical*. It isn't cosmetic. Resist boring a reader by describing the color of Betsy's hair or eyes. The color of her panties, perhaps scarlet, reveals more of her.

Characterization is also physical oddity.

In *Moby-Dick*, it is Captain Ahab's wooden leg. At night, as the young cabin boy lies awake in his bunk, he hears a thumping from above, as a sleepless Ahab paces the planks of his deck. To and fro drums a restless and resolute shipmaster who angers for revenge upon the great white whale.

In daytime, before an assembled crew, Ahab calls for nail and hammer, then pounds a gold piece to a mast . . . a bonus for the man who is first to sight Moby's blow.

Tools make *sound!*

Let your reader hear it, feel it; rattle his skull and bones with the beat of its poetry. Pierce his ears.

Your young hero is hired to work at a papermill, in the chipper room. Cordwood, all of which measures four feet in length, cascades into the chipper's gaping black maw, where giant spinning blades reduce each log to poker-chip size.

As a lad, I did this job for International Paper, at a very old mill in Ticonderoga. The noise is Hell on Earth. The dust tortures your nose, eyes, lungs. I worked an eight-hour tour. The mill never stops. Every third week, I worked the graveyard shift, 11:00 at night to 7:00 in the morning. Then, when my replacement reported drunk, my foreman let me work another eight hours.

I am now partially deaf.

Thus, when you write your story, let your reader hear the noise, the roar of that giant chipping machine, the vibration that almost gouges his guts.

The only tool he uses is a wood hook.

It's a single device. No more than a foot long, one cylindrical handle that's a bit more chunky than a roll of quarters, and a steel hook that sprouts from the handle's center like a question mark.

I've seen men fight with wood hooks. Shirts and flesh would tear and blood would gusher. Many of the men wore scars or grew beards to hide the shame of losing.

To sum it all up, use tools.

A man's ax (like a woman's needle) shows a reader what a character *does*. Your reader will decide, *without your assistance*, what kind of man he *is* . . . his beliefs, the devotions of his life that he holds dear.

In short, hand a young Jesus his mallet. Do so, and you'll surely charm at least two of your readers who revere His carpentry.

Billy Graham and me.

11
Dirt and Arnold Toynbee

Historians hate novelists.

But please, don't blame Arnold or the rest of the historians, because there is a very normal reason for their getting a bit huffy. It has to do with money and envy.

Perhaps historians resent us because we fiction writers write not for historians, but for history *buffs*. Considering this: My warped and twisted mind somehow envisions a swarm of unclad people pawing through a bookstore in search of *Fawn* or *Hang for Treason* or *Eagle Fur*. (Please note how cleverly I manage to name-drop the titles of my books at every opportunity. All writers should do this. After all, is Procter & Gamble reluctant to mention Tide or Crest?)

Novelists shamelessly crib from history books that are dull, write historical novels that are sexy and exciting, and rake in impressive incomes. Historians, on the other hand, hardly earn anything at all and dress like walking CARE packages. It often takes history profs decades to crank out *their* stuff. We novelists do ours while sliding down a firepole.

No wonder they envy us.

Are historians bitter about the speed of our typewriters? You bet your asterisk. In fact, they take out their frustrations by writing most of their history books in mouse-type footnotes.

Nonetheless, I like Arnold Toynbee because he said something once that, to me, makes sense . . . not just for history and sociology, but also for drama and comedy.

"Dirt," quoth Arnold, "is matter out of place."

That has to be one of the most profound statements I ever read and one of the few I ever understood. Think about it, please. Here's how:

Take every single article you own out of your house and heap it into one big pyramid in your front yard. Or dig up your entire front lawn and pile all the earth in your parlor. Either way, you'd have matter out of place. Dirt.

It is midnight, and I, Robert Newton Peck (a white guy) walk down a dimly lit sidestreet in New York's Harlem, a black neighborhood. I am whistling "Dixie." Also, I am foolishly being matter out of place. And, in a matter of only minutes, I will become personally involved in a drama.

It is General Custer and his cavalry riding into a bunch of whooping Sioux. This happened about the time Arnold Toynbee was born, so I doubt very much if Crazy Horse read much Toynbee. However, he acted. Crazy Horse spotted Custer, concluded that the bluecoats were matter out of place, seeing they were cantering on his turf, and did something about it.

Drama unfolded and Custer folded.

Now, had General Custer remained in the cozy safety of the fort, we wouldn't have had any excitement at all, readers would have had no drama, and Crazy Horse no scalps.

George Armstrong Custer at Little Big Horn, like Neil Armstrong, astronaut on the moon, is matter out of place. They were dramatic.

Comedy, as well as drama, is also matter out of place.

Comedy is a hippo in a pink tutu dancing *Swan Lake*. Howard Cosell *playing* football. Colonel Sanders as the guest of honor at the vegetarian picnic. Or a lawyer in Heaven.

An example of how matter out of place sparks comedy, please note *The Beverly Hillbillies* on TV . . . Tennessee mountaineers transplanted to posh Beverly Hills, California.

As I said in *Secrets of Successful Fiction*, writing is physics, moving parts, things. What matters is matter, like dirt. But what matters even more in comedy or drama is *where* the matter is.

Your job, as a fiction writer, is to uproot.

Grammar is placing proper words where they properly belong. Fiction is uprooting matter and transplanting it to where it does *not* belong. That's both drama and comedy.

Sometime do yourself a favor and read a novelette by Ernest Hemingway entitled *The Old Man and the Sea*. It's about an old fisherman who sails his boat out too far, to where he does not belong. He goes alone, without his usual boy for a helper, and he hooks a giant marlin. In my opinion, it is the best hooker story I ever read, as well as the most beautiful Christian allegory ever written in the English language.

Now then, you might begin to wonder, does all drama hinge on travel? No, not hardly.

The reverse also works. Your hero can stay at home, where life is absolutely peachy, but then trouble comes to him.

The plot of *Justice Lion* begins to hum when, during Prohibition, a federal agent, Elmer Sternlock, arrives in the small town of Liberty, Vermont, and pokes his nose where it doesn't belong . . . into the distilling of corn whiskey. Had not Mr. Sternlock come to Liberty, there would be no plot and no trial.

Sternlock is a minor character. Yet he is trouble come to town, the skunk at the lawn party, the catalyst, the spur that urges a town's sleepy trot into a thundering gallop. The rowels of Sternlock's determination rake the ribs of the residents.

Drama is discomfort.

 You, as a writer, must realize that a change of pace is called for to *churn* your homebound characters. Think of the people in a quiet little town, or community, as though they are inert curds inside an old-fashioned butter churn. Your curds cannot stay unmolested in there forever; if they do, no one will read your novel. It'll be creamy but dull.

Look! Coming over the horizon, heading toward us, rides the stranger on a black horse. To butter the bread of your book.

The beauty of this fellow is that he does *not* have to be a major character. *But* he does have to perform one very essential task. He climbs off his horse, flicks the reins over the hitching rail in front of the saloon, and shakes things up. Grabbing the handle of your butter churn, he pumps it up and down. If your story takes place in Turkey, the local Kurds are going crazy.

Is the stranger a bad guy or a good guy?

He can be either. Or, like most of us, a combination of good and evil . . . a human being, just doing his job, an Elmer Sternlock. The important thing is this: The stranger brings about *change*.

Learn this about folks. Most of us, I dare say all of us, resent change. Perhaps, at first, we laugh at the stranger in his odd clothes. Then, step two, we begin to fear him. Finally, we hate him. In many a primitive language, a linguist once told me, the word *stranger* means the same as *enemy*.

So, I beg of you, change either the geography or the situation. Somebody in your story has to leave the fort, like Custer; or come storming into town, like Elmer Sternlock. But not always. Not all books employ the stranger strategy. However, it is a tool for you, the writer, to consider using. It works.

When you are composing a list, a cast, of characters for your novel, at least consider adding a stranger. He is the waiter, if you'll pardon a pun, who serves a menu of variety to your table of content. Many times, who he is and what he does is not nearly as important as how your main stay-at-home characters *react* to his sudden entrance into the scene.

Emerging writers can sometimes tumble into what I call *the bowling alley trap*.

Picture, if you will, ten white bowling pins. They stand in a neat triangle, neither bruised nor molested, and will stand there forever until you, the bowling author, roll a ball down the boards. As a bowler, you hope the ball is going to mess up the formation and create a noise.

Question:

Do the pins know the ball is coming?

Do all your sweet and kindly characters in Niftyville know that Mean Malcolm is coming to town on the next stagecoach? Or does M.M. just show up and surprise everyone?

Next question:

Do we, the readers of your story, get to see Mean Malcolm *before* he arrives in town? If so, do we learn exactly what makes him so mean? An unhappy childhood perhaps. All the other children had red tricycles. Malcolm's was puce.

Explore as many possibilities as your brain can muster. For example, *why* is Mean Malcolm coming to Niftyville? Another consideration: Is Malcolm a stranger to everyone in town? Is there a gal there he loves? Or a man, now old, who presented him with his boyhood puce tricycle, which warped his life forever?

What I'm warning you about is this: Malcolm did *not* cover his eyes, circle a finger, and then touch Niftyville on a map. There has to be a *reason* for his coming.

This provides you yet another approach:

Everyone in Niftyville imagines, or concludes, that Mean Malcolm is coming to town for one reason. But, truth be known, he is actually coming for an entirely different purpose.

To conclude, it is going to be one heck of a boring evening if all the bowling pins continue to stand unmolested. And a very blah story.

So much of successful fiction hinges on one simple ploy: *disruption.* An impersonal bomb that drops on Niftyville is not nearly as exciting as, to be momentarily charitable, the coming of personable Malcolm. Because he is a human being and fiction is folks.

Making our Malcolm a stranger, instead of just the ornery chap who lives over on Maple Avenue, adds a wisp of mystery to your cast of characters. He is the fellow we *don't know*. He doesn't belong in Niftyville, yet we wonder if any local champion will have the bowels to tell him so and persuade Malcolm to wave bye-bye and split.

The *stranger* element among your folks is a useful tool. Use it. Because, as Mean Malcolm rides into town on his black stallion, he is matter out of place. He is dirt.

Arnold Toynbee, ya done good.

12
Buzz
Words

Please allow me to err.

(I think it was Mae West who said, "To err is human, but it feels divine.")

This chapter on buzz words obviously doesn't belong, at first glance, in a book that supposedly deals with characterization. But I want to shoehorn it in, right now and early on, because I want to point out to you that Arnold Toynbee's "matter out of place" also can be useful for *phrases* as well as *folks*.

This may irk my beloved editors but thank goodness it won't bother you. Just think of this chapter as a postscript for Arnold.

On second thought, a chapter on buzz words *does* belong in this book. Why? Because you can use them when you write dialogue as well as narrative, and dialogue is very much a tint of characterization.

What people say is part of what they are.

If a character of yours speaks in color (as opposed to colorlessly), the buzz words of his dialogue tend to brighten your tale.

So here goes:

One word can save a sentence.

The sentence you just read, obviously, has not been saved at all. It is boring and dies a horrible death at the hands of this writer. It's dull. But let's give it another go.

One word can *gussy up* a sentence.

Sometimes, all a sentence needs to brighten it is just one little buzz word. That one unexpected blast is the pothole in fiction's road. An awkward word to *hopscotch* a reader's eye. And thus, tickle a fancy.

A buzz word is matter out of place. It doesn't belong there. Yet, without it, the entire sentence is about as exciting as opening night at the You-Scrub-It Car Wash. Buzz words are misfits.

Now comes the key question. How does a writer's brain conjure up a buzz word?

Easy.

Perhaps not a piece of cake but surely it can be a *slab* of pie.

My secret is to personalize the intangible. Introduce the action of some living thing, a person or plant or animal, and discover how this living thing acts out the intangible word.

Explanation: Tangible words are *chair, horse, ball, hat, bicycle.* Intangible words (which should be avoided unless you want your writing to bore readers as well as editors) are *beauty, nature, love, hate, mean, happy, sad,* and *hope.*

Let's take an intangible word: *success.*

By itself, *success* splotches no color for the reader's picture-hungry eye. But add a person's ego to it and you'll personalize it into the *swagger* of success. Or the *strut* of confidence.

A sunrise at dawn shows light and color. But does it make any noise? To my ear, yes. An early sun is the golden *gong* of morning.

Gong is the buzz word, the unexpected noun (please note that it is stronger than an adjective) that jolts. It doesn't quite fit. I like it, even though the sun is not a musical instrument any more than the moon is a form of food. When a full midnight moon is a silver *wafer*, your sentence buzzes.

The wrong of it (like the gong of it) reads so right.

If gong reads too Oriental for your Western eye, please remember that a sunrise is an Eastern scene.

Recently, the young son of a dear friend of mine was killed in a car crash. In the eulogy that I gave at the funeral service, I described the boy's brief life as a mere *trinket* of time.

At a funeral, the word *trinket* sounds like matter out of place. Too cosmetic. As I wrote the eulogy, I almost scratched it out because one cannot talk of jewelry at such a tragic moment. The word stared up at me, looking shallow and brittle, almost ashamed of itself. Yet I allowed it to stay.

One time, I heard a Bible verse described as a *scrap* of Scripture. It rings. Such out-of-place buzz words, like ragtime, break the cadence. And mend boredom.

During a speech before an adoring audience, I informed the crowd that despite literary and television success, I was still a simple Vermont country boy. "I love the humble sounds of Nature," I told them, "like the tap of a raindrop . . . on the roof . . . of my Rolls."

Sometimes (as seen above) set-up lines have to be used to roll out a lush red carpet . . . for a *hobo* to parade on.

Do you enjoy a surprise?

I do.

So do lots of readers. As do editors. That's all a buzz word is, a surprise. Its structure is basically pictorial. Sneakers beneath a tuxedo. The old-fashioned giant tail fins of a car that propel it along, like *whale flukes*. Matter out of place.

One flashing *red light* of guilt.

So don't hesitate to *tin* a reader's ear. It will charm his eye.

"The farmer looked at the sky to see the dark clouds *breeding* weather."

Clouds, poor devils, don't really *breed*. Yet that one uncomfortable buzz verb puts a burr into the bouquet. The tired cliché would be *threatening clouds*, two words that you have read on scores of pages.

Speaking of sky . . .

Ideas come down from above? No.

Ideas *beam* down.

Here's an exercise:

Pump life into each sentence by changing one word. Make it a clumsy word, a pothole . . . a word that pertains to *folks*. A living word instead of a dead one.

George heard the insult.

George felt the *swat* of insult.

Okay, so I changed more than one word. Nobody's perfect.

Picture your sentence as a sleepy herd of beef cows. You're the cowboy. Suddenly one little stray bolts away from the rest of your cattle. That single stray is the critter that you and your horse now pursue. You don't look at the others. They're all in place. It's the *maverick* you're after.

Buzz words are mavericks.

To a reader's eye, the buzzer breaks away from the other sleepy words and, behold, you have etched a picture. A scene. Your sentence is now, because of a wayward maverick, active, not passive.

Buzzers are alive.

They have movement, smell, touch (swat), taste, and sound. And it takes only one buzz word to *pepper* the meal. In your hand, you now hold a Rubik's cube. On one surface you see nine tiny squares. Eight of them are yellow. One is *red*. Which one are you looking at?

The wonderful fact about buzz words is that you already know all the ones that you'll ever need to use.

But don't overuse them!

Ofttimes, a simple and pure declarative sentence will serve your fiction better than if you're straining constantly to be clever. Remember that your readers may not be quite as chic as you and they may resent your intrepid grunts for glorification.

To put it another way, do not have your hero overworking his cleverness in his dialogue. Few of us are delightful with every word we speak. So be sure that the folks in your fiction are true to life in this respect. Then, when the reader's guard is down, uppercut his eye with a jolting buzzer.

Where do you find buzz words?

Easy.

They are potentially everywhere. Here's the method I use to zing a buzzword into my pages:

Take a cliché, a phrase that we all use repeatedly and is familiar to the eyes and ears of the world. There! I just used one! All you do now is warp it a bit, add to it, tinker with a word here and there, and you'll create a buzzer.

By itself, *the eyes and ears of the world* is neither clever nor refreshing. But when a renowned allergist bills herself as "the eyes, ears, nose, and throat of the world," it's unique.

Remember, it doesn't have to be a real thigh-slapper.

A buzz word, or phrase, can also soften that which was formerly harsh. It can be kind and loving as well as comic. Also, it can be poetic. On the other hand, it can be critical, even cynical.

I once described a college prof, a fellow whom I like a lot, addressing his class in a discussion of one of my early novels, *A Day No Pigs Would Die*. At the time, I happened to be a nervous guest in his literary classroom. The prof then proceeded to dissect my book as though it were a cadaver. He held on high its chapters, like cold organs, and then gutted it.

He did, however, reassemble my novel before the class was over, and even made the prediction that "the patient would live and *endearingly endure.*"

Needless to add, the buzz word that will smirk your ego the most (clever you!) is the word twist at the end of one of your sentences. Whenever I do this in a book, my pen almost struts as I write, arrogant tool that it is.

When socialite Miss Daphne DeBenture Dow-Jones threw a party, her engraved invitations requested that all the girls attend the dance in white gowns. Daphne, however, shockingly appeared in pink. No fool she. "It's my party," she said, "and I'll shine if I want to."

Needless to add, without Daphne's sly (dare I say color-scheming?) trickery, her shindig would have been just one more cotillion. No matter if all the other young ladies were blandly white with envy.

Daphne was the belle of the *brawl*.

13

The Mosquito Quotient

You're almost asleep.

Then you detect a soft, high-pitched whine, and it seems to be coming closer and closer to your exposed ear. It's a bug. You know that a mosquito has invaded your bedroom, and sleep will be impossible until you nail him with your slipper.

You flick on a light. You're going to whack that bug if it's the last thing you ever do.

This midnight scene is one of the secrets of plot.

More important, it's also the basis of characterization. Many a thrilling yarn is begun by somebody who *bugs* somebody else.

What bugs you?

Chances are, the circumstances and the *folks* who annoy you, and all readers, are the kinds of pests that pester characters. So, let's look at a few pestering-festering situations.

Are there currently so many young hooligans in your neighborhood that you deny yourself the pleasure of an evening stroll for fear of getting mugged, and it bugs you?

Do you purchase a gun, even though you've never liked

firearms and in your entire life never owned one? More and more people are doing this. Pistol ranges abound these days. Prevention outweighing cure. The rape prevented beats the rape reported.

What else bugs you?

Have you, if you're a woman, suffered menstrual pain since age thirteen; and every doctor either smirks or prescribes a placebo, a sugar pill?

Because of the cost of today's housing, do you live so far away from your job that it almost requires an extra shift, in rush hour traffic, just to commute?

Does a repairman fix one gadget while breaking two?

How about the chap who used to live in your house and moved to Tibet without ever telling you where the septic tank is buried? It isn't a whole lot of fun to probe for it and succeed only in punching a hole in one of the soft pipes of your sprinkler system.

Who lives next door?

Is it young Nerdy Nuisance who is a hi-fi nut and plays rock music at an electric-chair voltage level?

Why can't Edsel, your oldest son, ever get along in school? You've tried to help him with his algebra but he tells you not to bug him. And his room has the fragrance of an old sneaker.

Maybe your job's killing you.

Perhaps, at times of mindless rage, you'd like to murder your boss. Or just run away to Acapulco with your leggy secretary, Bathsheba Biltmore, who types twenty errors into every business letter and knows you could never fire a fox with legs that long.

All the rest of the people in your department at the office, call you Mr. Studwell . . . but Bathsheba abbreviates your name whenever your door is closed and then slowly crosses her legs. She refuses to wear hose because it's July and her limbs are very tan.

"It's a bikini tan," says Bathsheba, leaving her complete anatomical nomenclature up to your wildest glandular speculation.

Bathsheba seems jittery today.

Her steady boyfriend, she explains, is away for the summer and she's climbing the walls.

She bugs you, eh? Worse yet, Bathy knows she's doing it. And you know she knows. On top of all that, every other guy in the office keeps telling you what a lucky guy you are to have Miss Biltmore for a secretary.

As they do it, they wink.

Your boss, Mr. T.J. Bigdesk, has noticed her also. And has no doubt compared Bathy to *his* secretary, Miss Witherfork, who has been with the company since it was originally founded, about the time of Stonehenge.

Other matters bug you. Serious ones.

Your closest friend in the company, Sam Scott, is worried because his wife is ill. The sales curve takes a downward elbow and T.J. fires Sam.

As you watch Sam cleaning out his desk, you're tempted to crash into the boss's office and tell him off. You even take a step toward T.J.'s door. Your mind starts forming the words you want to say. He'll be busy, as usual, behind his big desk.

"What do *you* want?" he might ask.

"Well," you could explain, "I just popped in to ruin my career and tell you that you're making one heck of a big mistake to fire Sam Scott."

T.J. would remove his glasses.

"Yeah?" you imagine his saying.

Can you do it?

If you don't do it, will your own cowardice *bug* you for the rest of your life? And if you do it, will T.J. give you the ax, the pink slip? Two of your three kids need braces on their teeth and all three will want a college education. Your wife, only this morning, said that the car's transmission is shot, according to Gus at the service station.

You recall an old adage. Sometimes the boss is right. Sometimes the boss is wrong. But the boss is *always* the *boss.*

"You can't afford to get fired, so don't be a sucker," the weakling in you whispers.

Then you shake hands with Sam, tell him that the office won't be the same without his jokes, and that even though he's fifty-six he'll be able to land another job.

Lying bugs you.

You walk Sam Scott as far as the elevator. Out of respect for old times. He tells you that he'd been with the company for over twenty-five years. That's when you remember that Sam was the guy who, many years ago, hired *you.*

Back then, you hadn't had much experience. Your resumé was thin, unimpressive. Sam had looked at you, grinned, and said that he'd take a chance and give you a job.

The gang at the office always agreed that Sam Scott was a great guy to work for. Never leaned on you without a reason, a good one.

Doors on the elevator close. Sam's gone.

On the way back to your office, you notice T.J.'s door. Still closed tightly. The boss does this when he doesn't want to be disturbed or when he's dictating.

Heck with it! You'll just interrupt him. Barge in and ask him why he fired Sam. You tell yourself it's your right to know.

Your hand touches the big brass knob of his big oaken door. It feels hard.

All you have to do now is turn it, open the door, and be the only guy in the office who has guts enough to stand up for Sam Scott, the man who hired you. The only thought that stops you is paying for a new transmission for the car. And then paying the dentist. Plus saving enough for a vacation trip to the mountains, for five people and a dog.

You've promised the family they'll go.

So you walk away from the boss's door, back to your own office, knowing that you'll wonder forever if you'll ever be a man.

Things that bug you deeply are probably the same ones that bug the rest of us. Burrs under humanity's saddle. And it's easier to sell a book to a publisher when the horse is bucking. What bugs you bugs characters and bucks up a plot.

Now then, why did I suddenly take off on one particular

bug, the office scene when T.J. fires Sam Scott? I'll tell you why. I probably don't have to because you're bright (you bought this book, didn't you?) and you've already guessed. It's because Studwell, the hero, is sensitive to someone else's discomfort and not to only his own.

That is the acid test for bugs, which decides whether one particular bug will blossom into a story.

Are you bugged because someone else is in pain, has been fired, has been robbed or raped or ripped off? If so, then you might have yourself a hero.

I'll tell you, point blank, when you do *not* have a hero. It is when your leading character is concerned only with himself, his life, his comfort or discomfort. I, for one, don't hanker to read much more than a paragraph about some self-centered egotist who is totally unaware that other people can feel even a slight twinge of distress.

Okay, your hero Studwell is aware.

But is that enough? Doesn't he want to *do* something about it? Yet the action isn't immediate. There has to come an inner struggle, Studwell versus Studwell, as he weighs the possibilities of following Sam Scott out into the jobless street.

Who will win?

Will it be Ivanhoe Studwell, a knight at arms, protector of the discharged . . . or will it be Sir Studwell the Survivor?

To be realistic, only in the movies will Studwell tell T.J. Bigdesk that he, the boss, made a mistake. In your office and mine, people don't have the guts for glory. They've sold their souls for the paycheck.

Hold it!

Let's back up a pace or two. All right, we'll both admit that there isn't much moral courage in humanity. But perhaps, in your story, there should be some. A novel can stretch up higher than life. Perhaps our hero Studwell does drum up his guts, invades T.J.'s office and asks him to hire back Sam. Or he quits.

Can you allow T.J. Bigdesk to change his decision and rehire Sam Scott? No, you cannot. Bosses don't do this. Not a single corporate executive I know would allow Studwell to pressure him. Bigdesk may admire Stud's courage but not his judgment. The only logical outcome is that Mr. Studwell will be fired too.

That's what happens. Studwell gets the ax.

Now, if you're to be a writer, you must use a long blade to carve deeply into a situation. Conduct exploratory surgery, to look for possible situations, varying ways for your plot to turn and twist.

Now we'll twist the knife.

Following the firing of Studwell, good old Sam Scott hears about it, goes to Mr. Bigdesk, and contracts to fill Studwell's vacant post. Bigdesk, being somewhat desperate for personnel (now missing two men) hires Sam back.

Well, does Studwell learn of this?

He almost has to. Does he shrug it off, tell Sam off, or what? Perhaps he learned that Bigdesk, because of a budget cut, was forced by upper management to let one salesman go. And it had to be Studwell or Sam Scott.

Does he meet Sam, by accident, on the street? If so, will Sam suddenly jaywalk to avoid a confrontation, and then does Stud give chase? Sam *runs*. By the way, does Studwell know that Sam Scott has a serious heart condition? As he runs, what happens to Sam's heart as a result of this sudden panic and exertion, plus the tensions of his getting fired and then rehired?

Is there a physical struggle?

Not important. What is pivotal is the internal struggle that Studwell has with himself, over whether he is knight or toady. Now you've finally discovered the real *bug* of the novel.

It isn't Sam's getting the ax that really digs into Studwell's mind. Instead, it is wondering if he, Studwell, is really a man. Amazing, is it not? All these notes, endless possibilities, and then . . . *pow!* You suddenly realize what the core of your story really is. It is not about an uncaring boss who fires a friend. It is not about the fact that the friend sneaks back to claim your former job.

It's about manhood.

And it is a universal and critical question in the mind of many a male. "Am I a real man?" This is why weak men slap women and abuse children. Because they have yet to prove their masculinity.

Now then, we have produced a problem. It is this: Is it legitimate for Studwell's noble concern for Sam Scott to abandon its course, turning inward, to kick up doubts of masculinity? Perhaps not. Earlier, we said that self-concern made boring characters. Yet, to show you how there are few rules for fiction, we all are truly concerned about survival.

As you write this story, your story, or any story, don't decide too early how it shall end. Please do not. Because, as you write, certain quirks and traits of your characters may *bug* you. The slightest annoyance can, under certain strained circumstances, nudge a tiller and thereby alter the novel's direction.

Wars can start over one pesky incident.

So heed the mosquito in the night. You'll have to. Because no mosquito, like no fictional possibility, however small, can go ignored. Do so and your readers will stay up with you.

They'll be reading your books.

14
How to Kick a Dead Lion

I have a black friend.

His name is Jethro Brown and he's a truck driver who beats me at chess. In the formal sense, Jeth has had almost no education. Yet he enjoys reading books.

He reads all of mine; which will, perhaps, label Jethro as a man whose tastes could stand some upgrading.

One of Jethro's many interests is Africa.

He's a whiz at African lore; collects spears. He also shared an ancient African folktale with me. A story, according to Jeth, that is very old and well known in many tongues.

"It's about a lion and a coward," said Jethro. "And the first barefoot kicker."

Centuries ago, a small village in Africa had been molested by a lion. He was a loner, no longer king of a pride, meaning he had no females to hunt for him. As he had grown old, survival meant preying upon the cattle and the children of the village.

Grabbing their spears, the courageous hunters of the village ventured forth. All the men went, except one man, because he was afraid to go.

They killed the lion.

As they dragged the carcass back to the village, everyone was cheering. Children were now brave enough to venture close to touch the dead animal. The coward finally came too. And kicked it.

You, as a writer, can make professional use of Jethro Brown's story of a coward and a lion.

Cowards make fascinating characters. They abound. You see them on TV and you read their articles in newspapers and magazines. They almost always talk and write after the fact.

For example, Richard Nixon, in the political sense, is a dead lion. Yet the cowards are still kicking, no longer remembering when he was king of the pride. They voted for him, too. Facts so indicate. Because when President Nixon ran for a second term, after four years in the White House, he carried forty-nine out of fifty states.

The old lion, now in his seventies, still receives kick upon kick. He was never my personal hero. Yet I believe that our Lord's Prayer promises forgiveness to us all. And this includes old lions.

My point, dear emerging writer, is that you can flush a coward out from under every bush. Such a coward isn't much of a man—or woman. But a coward sure can furnish your novel with one super character.

So use him.

Where do you find such a fellow?

We have only to look to ourselves; for inside each of us lurks a coward as well as a hero. We're humans all, baffling blends of Woody Allen and John Wayne, little and large.

When I was a soldier, in Italy, at age seventeen, there was a guy in my outfit who loudly claimed that he wasn't afraid to die. Maybe *he* wasn't, but I sure was. Rob Peck was scared out of his skull. Inside, I was the biggest coward who ever paraded in a U.S. Army uniform.

I'll tell you a sad story.

Years and years ago, when my income was a buck or two less than modest, I lived in a congested neighborhood of small houses and lots of kids.

One morning, on a Saturday, a dog was hit by a car.

The driver, loaded perhaps with something other than empathy, never even stopped. He left the dog to die. In less than a minute, a crowd of perhaps a hundred parents and children gathered around the bloody animal whose intestines had been entirely ruptured from his crushed body.

The animal yelped in unbearable agony. Everyone was talking, knowing something had to be done. I killed the dog with one blow of an ax.

The entire crowd gasped in shock. No one could speak. But as I dragged the dead animal away, to dig a hole to dignify its death, I heard one woman make a remark. She didn't like me and here was her chance.

"He *would* do something like that."

My point is this: Even inside a coward like me there abides a dormant George who taps my shoulder to urge, "Do it."

The crux of *Kirk's Law* is just such a situation. It's about a boy who realizes that action is called for, *now*, and there's no one else to tackle the job. He is George.

In other words, your coward character is not a person of singular dimension. Not simple. Complicated! There are reasons for his cowardice and your readers deserve to know them. Perhaps he had once been brave, foolishly so, and the scar still lashes at his memory.

Deepen his personality.

Shakespeare, in *Macbeth*, shows us two killers at dawn. They are cowards, lying in wait to pounce on their victim. Yet their words to one another are poetic. The Bard gave verse to vermin.

We all fear.

Be honest, therefore, with thyself. What causes *you* to be afraid? Darkness? Water? Crowds? Your boss? Does fear of getting fired goose your bumps? Does the thought of your husband's mother who is coming to visit for a month (or only for dinner) rattle your ribs?

In the mind of every young mother lurks the potential disapproval of the girl whom her adorable Basil is going to wed.

Guess what? You're the girl.

Basil's at work, the doorbell is ringing, and you know it's Basil's mummy. Too late—you've already discovered how she'd spoiled your hubby rotten, and she's fully prepared to warn you that turnips never fail to upset Basil's gourmet standards, and disrupt the sensitivities of his lower digestive tract.

Mummy is even going to tell you this during dinner, as Basil forks the grub into his delicate belly with all the mealtime charm of a Cro-Magnon. As he belches, Mom will blame the turnips and you.

Do you want to tell Mummy something?

On the tip of your tongue, is there suddenly one cute little cutter to convince Mummy to at least *swallow* before riposting? Don't worry. Basil won't hear. He's up to his ears in turnips.

Well, my coward, are you going to say it?

Cowardice, you see, is comic as well as tragic. There's *fun* in it, too. It boils, like a turnip, right down to this: Your characters are people like you. And me. So are your readers. They fully know what joy it is to be Basil's wife and they also want to add arsenic to Mummy's meal.

In our own little lives, we readers are a tad too timid to poison the Mummy of the family and then be haunted by Mummy's ghost.

So *you* have to do it.

It's up to you, as a writer, to design a cowardly character who dasn't dare tell Mummy to stick her turnips where the sun don't shine. Or sprinkle the strychnine on her sprouts.

Ah, the coward's agony.

Your readers will know, and identify, because they've all been there and back. When it's too late, as dear Basil is asleep and snoring off his half-ton dinner, you're lying awake, thinking of all the rippy remarks that you wished you'd made to Mummy. To settle her hash.

So, punching your pillow, you merely roll over and pretend you're saying them now. You're kicking a dead lion.

Jethro Brown told us how.

15
Skunks and Reactionaries

As a boy I had a pet skunk.

Her name was Zebra. Like most skunks, she was striped black and white, softer than flour, and graced with a very pleasant disposition.

A neighbor's dog made a big mistake with Zebra. He concluded that her sweet and quiet nature was an indication of cowardice. Oh, how wrong he was! Awesome weaponry ensures a skunk, like a nation, the right to live a peaceful and gentle life, unmolested by Russians or Rover.

Skunks are reactionaries.

If you're a writer, allow Rob Peck to add that a human reactionary is even more useful to your cast of characters. Ergo, to the entire thrust of your novel.

Plots evolve from *reaction* as much as action.

Before we go any further, let's get one thing straight. The *reactionary* I'm about to examine for you is not political. Sometimes the unwise among us use the term too loosely, telling us that a reactionary is a wild-eyed right-winger who wants to thwart lofty liberal goals. They claim he starts trouble.

Hogwash.

A *reactionary* is as the term clearly states. He is not a person who originally acts. Instead, he *reacts*.

He's a counter-puncher.

If left to live unmolested, the reactionary, Lord bless him, minds his own business, hoes his own potatoes, and is a good, solid, responsible, self-centered citizen. Pays taxes. Helps his neighbor. Charity, as he sees it, is voluntary and not mandatory.

Let's name him Larry Little.

Larry's forty-three, goes to church with Myrna and the kids about eleven times a year, and works at Midas Muffler. He watches TV a lot and goes bowling with the guys every Wednesday night.

At the muffler shop, workdays are noisy enough, so Larry likes peace and quiet. Oh, maybe after his shift is over, he'll stop in at Mulligan's Bar & Grill and swill down a suds or two. But he won't start a fight. Not even when some loudmouth claims that the Steelers, his favorite football team, won't go to the Super Bowl.

Larry's no bully.

The last punch he threw was away back in high school, at a dance, and it was over Myrna. He married her when they were both nineteen. Two of their four kids are grown and have left home. The younger two are still in school.

Over on Elm Street, behind where the Littles live on their quarter-acre, there's an empty lot. Larry grew up only five doors from where he now resides and used to play ball in that lot. Back then, kids called it The Lot. Today's kids still do.

Nobody seems to know who owns it.

Until a sign goes up. The Lot, so the sign announces, has been purchased by Union City Realty and will be the future property of Ibex Industries, a foreign-controlled conglomerate of which neither the Littles nor their neighbors have ever heard.

"What's a ibex?" Larry asks Bud at the shop.

Bud shrugs. "It beats me. Alice said she heard it was something like a goat. Perhaps what they're fixing to do there is make toy goats or something. Maybe goat food."

On Sunday, Bud comes over from next door to watch TV football with Larry. He brings a six-pack. At halftime, they get to talking, worry some, and try to finger Ibex in the phone book. Nothing. And no listing for Union City *anything*.

"Alice says she heard in the supermarket that they're planning to knock down all them big trees."

Larry sighs. "They shouldn't let 'em do that."

"Yeah. Remember our tree house?"

"I sure do." Larry nods. "Nobody could forget that."

Bud taps Larry's knee with an empty Blatz can. "Another thing Alice picked up. They're gonna build a access road, across the back, which'll cut off a strip of our property. Yours too."

Larry frowns. "They can't do that." He scratches himself with a thick hand. "Can they?"

"Maybe we oughta see a lawyer."

"Nuts to that. All them guys do is talk and take your money. Judges, too. A judge is just a lawyer in a black dress who's got a political connection."

"They're gonna take a slice of our lots, Larry."

"Who says?"

"Some fancy law. My sister, Eunice, used to do half-day typing down at the court house. She says they can do it legal. It's called purparty. And I guess it means the city can approve any road they want, even if it cuts through a church."

Larry throws his beer can. "No! They ain't gonna cut off *my* backyard. I got rights."

"They can do it legal, Eunice says. She claims they done it over on McCoy Avenue, when they put in the new sewer main."

Larry Little smacks a hand with a fist. "They, they, *they*. Who in hell are these *they* people that got all the rights? *They* ain't even got no lousy *phone*."

On the floor lies an open telephone directory which Larry kicks, tearing a page.

Please note that Larry Little does not start the trouble. But soon his back will arch, as Zebra's did against the dog; and *they* who try to push him, crowd him, take away a hunk of his quarter-acre, are in for a battle.

Beware.

Larry Little is about to *react*.

He isn't big, rich, or educated. Larry is you and me. Just folks. Content, until *they* come along to tread on his toes. Not a seeker of status but a keeper of the status quo. Things as they are. The Lot is being raped. Big friendly trees bulldozed down. Its meadow paved. But the camel straw is purparty . . . a slice of his property going to some Ibex guy that Larry Little never heard of.

Right now, Larry's face is reddening.

Please note here that our issue is *territorial;* thus, extremely basic. Universal to all of life in our bio world. I want you to read a book I wrote, closely associated with Larry Little's problem, entitled *Path of Hunters*. It is not about humans; yet it is, because it touches, and threatens, the habitats of wild animals.

After reading it, and, I hope, finding it to your intellectual or poetic liking, you may wish to dig deeper into Mother Nature and her property rights. If so, please allow me to suggest your reading *one* of these two: *African Genesis* or *The Territorial Imperative*.

I ask you to do this because, as Rob Peck sees it, the most important human right is a property right. It's turf. Money is not what socialism or fascism tries to take away from us first. No indeed. Initially, an evil government grabs our *land* and then our *weapons*, and our deeds.

Human rights have nothing to do with words, civil law, or our Constitution. As I see it, human rights come directly from God. *Territory, weaponry,* and one's *hoard* are merely three of many.

I hope, for their sake, the Ibex folks don't mess with Larry's castle. It may be a mess already, but at least it's *his* mess. His and Myrna's. As the unknown antagonists in the corporate towers of Union City and Ibex Industries close in on Larry, he becomes a protagonist.

He reacts.

The sword that a sudden circumstance presses into his hand he now wields—not for booty but for safety. Not an attacker. A protector. And the closer the fight advances toward his humble doorstep, the more ferociously he wages his war.

I like characters like Larry.

Speaking as both writer and human being, there is, I truly believe, something quite noble about the little gentleman who won't be bullied. Millions of readers will identify with him, and with my pet skunk, Zebra.

As I reread this chapter, I'm happy. Why? Because, as I wrote it, I got carried away. My spirit was swept into the current of Larry Little and his cause.

This is exactly what *you* must do.

Get carried away! Be enthusiastic about your characters. You don't write with pen but with *passion*. Which now brings us to a very useless question, one that you yourself may already be asking me:

"Where do I find a Larry?"

Needless to say, we all know him by another name. He lives next door, down the street, at your factory or office, or back in your old hometown.

Larry Little lives inside *you*.

He is the spirit within you that hollers, "Hey! Hold on a minute. You people aren't going to push me around or bully me." When you read your morning newspaper, read the letters to the editor.

Who writes them?

If you read even one, you'll know. Citizens, like you and me, the Larry Littles of your community. Folks who are upset about something that is happening and they don't like it.

After all, you have to be more than a mite huffy to take the time and patience to compose a letter to a newspaper editor. It's more than just an insult you yell out of your car window at another motorist. Why? Because *your name* is on the letter. That's why.

A letter isn't just a crude finger gesture to society. It's so very much more. A wrong has been committed and you're out to right it—and write it.

That quiet "Letters to the Editor" page in your newspaper is a super source for *issues* to write about, as well as a place to spy characters that are so irate they're already knee-deep involved. Involved? They are steaming!

Warning:

Don't just read the letters of anger.

Also, on that same page, you'll find a note from a subscriber who is sweet, kind, helpful—and, most endearingly of all, grateful. Most of us are combinations of emotion. Luckily, above many a hot collar there rests a cool head, waiting for everything below to simmer down and embrace reason.

But cool reason, lofty though she may be, isn't enough for a novel. Somebody's got to get really *ticked.*

Lots of times, it will be someone who doesn't start the trouble, yet somebody willing to wade in, answering a bugle's call to battle. These, for my dough, make the best folks in fiction. The little citizen, who wants only to be let alone to sip life's libation, is suddenly molested.

Molested by what? *Change!*

The pattern of his life is altered, his sweet and familiar path obstructed, and so he gets hot over a hurdle. The ordinary citizen, like Larry, will become your fiction's champion.

Larry Little will valiantly defend that wee patch of turf, called *home,* and I, for one, will cheer.

16
Daisies and Bathless Bart

When I was a kid, movies cost a dime.

Even so, back in those Great Depression days when dimes were hard to come by, Soup and I could somehow scrounge up two.

Saturday afternoons meant double features, B movies, or even C. One of the two pictures was always a cowboy thriller that pitted a hero against a villain.

Gene Autry versus Bathless Bart.

As we sat *glued* (because of discarded gum from previous occupants) to our seats, Soup and I knew that Gene was all good and Bathless Bart entirely bad. Gene always won, rounding up the rustlers as easily as he twanged out a tune.

However, in your book, please let Peck advise you to let Bathless Bart pick a daisy, hold it gently in his hairy paw, and admire its beauty.

Villains have souls.

Bart, like you and me, may not be all roses. Yet he's also not all cactus.

Oh, he's a rawhide rascal. No doubt about that. But if you

make Bathless Bart act mean merely because he *is* mean, your characterization will not ring true. He'll be about as believable as a senator explaining Chappaquiddick.

A memorable scoundrel, in my opinion, must act more out of hurt than just as a manifestation of his own cussedness.

I want you to read *Clunie.*

It's a very short little book about a retarded teenage girl, Clunie Finn. Perhaps, as you read it, you'll decide that the protagonist is not the young hero, Braddy Macon, who befriends Clunie, but rather Leo Bannon, who torments her.

Why is Leo so heartless?

He is not ungifted. Leo is a good baseball player and has been elected captain of his high school team. He's physically strong and not ugly in appearance. His bitterness stems from poverty and social rejection.

The reader feels Leo's hurt as the lad stands alone, in the darkness, outside a posh home where Sally Rowe, a haughty high school beauty, is hostessing a birthday party.

Leo Bannon was not invited.

He aches for Sally Rowe, cannot have her for a girlfriend, and so targets his hunger at someone he imagines is a more accessible young lady, Clunie Finn. As a result, Leo becomes a sad boy attempting an even sadder act. The scale of his feelings is rife with sharps and flats—shards of anger, coupled with his moments, at the town dump, of illusion and despair.

The tragedy is as much Leo's as it is Clunie's.

There exists a bit of Leo Bannon in all of us. Often we are tempted to shake a fist at circumstance that has dealt us the deuces of injustice. Self-pity, sometimes followed by the urge to get even, wells up in the human spirit, as lofty ambition sours and society points a finger to chuckle.

I believe that villainy sprouts from frustration and its revenge.

Ask yourself, as you create your own Leo and the facets of his nature, *what has he failed at?* Why are his goalposts so distant? Is he dirty, lazy, dumb, arrogant, greedy, jealous . . . or warped because of some failed experiment in his life that squelched promise?

Did someone else reap all the credit from the straight rows of his hoe and his sweat?

The question you just read applies to one of the great soldiers of the American Revolution, a man named Benedict Arnold. He whipped the British general, Burgoyne, at Saratoga. Credit went to another. Arnold became bitter and decided on revenge, to turn West Point over to the redcoats.

You know the story's outcome.

Still and all, Ben Arnold was one heck of a solid soldier. Few men who served with him ever doubted his brilliance or his courage. So I admire him for what he was and resent what he became, a traitor.

I'm not concerned whether or not Benedict Arnold was ever duly punished. No doubt his own torment lashed his conscience, until his death, ripping brass buttons from the tunic of his self-esteem. His sword was broken, I imagine, across the knee of regret.

Benedict Arnold's ragtag army was little more than a collection of farmboys with rabbit muskets, underfed and ill-paid. Yet with it, Arnold gave General John Burgoyne's regulars one rapturous licking.

Although it is an impossible longing, I wish I could have knelt at Arnold's bedside, as he died, if only to tell him, "Well done, sir." And to raise my hand to him in one final salute.

As I write about folks, I get carried away, don't I?

That's exactly what I want *you* to do. Fall in love, with a Leo or a Benedict or some Bathless Bart of your own imagination.

Honor the devil a bit.

If he's human, there's some noble stuff in him somewhere, because that's the formula God used when She gave birth to us all.

I sincerely believe that God loves all living things, including scorpions. So must authors. Hating your villain will not prosper you any more than hating your neighbor or your boss.

Perhaps, years ago, when the movie camera on the set had stopped cranking, Gene Autry and Bathless Bart laughed together and traded jokes. Gene maybe even wailed him a song.

If jolly old Gene can do it, so can you. Hand your Bart a daisy.

He deserves it.

If your novels are to be believed and admired, you can't create a hero, a Ludlow Goodpants, who is totally good and pure. Nobody (including the sages of Doubleday) will buy it.

Ergo, you cannot create a villain who is entirely bad. How are villains created?

They are sired by frustration.

George, let's say, wants Alice, who is sweet on Norman. George is not really a bad sort of a fellow. Yet, as he sits alone in the dark of a movie theater and observes Norman nuzzling delectable Alice, bitter jealously may ensue. Suddenly he may twist his empty popcorn box into tatters.

To make matters (or tatters) worse, both Norm and George work for the Gorilla Wrecking Company. Norman, because his last name is Gorilla (and he is also the boss's nephew) gets promoted to foreman.

Both of the lads live on Elm Street. And, on late summer evenings, as George tries to sleep in the darkness of his lonely room, he hears Norman strolling home after a date with Alice. Norm is whistling, skipping, and outwardly manifesting all indications that he enjoyed an evening of total gratification.

Norman also buys, on his new, improved foreman's salary, a new car. It's a red Vroom XKG, and he beeps the horn at George (who drives a used Toyota) as he and Alice go tooling by.

Alice, a few months back, used to date George. But no longer. Now her love life is Norman the Foreman. She, George fears, has desires to become Mrs. Norman Percival Gorilla.

Allow me also to add that George is exactly five feet tall. Norman is eight-foot three.

George cannot sleep at night,because, for some odd reason, he constantly envisions Alice in the long arms of Norman, as the two of them sit cozily together on the porch swing of Alice's shadowy veranda and engage in what used to be called a friendly exchange of slap and tickle.

George isn't tickled. He's ticked.

Is he itching to do something mean to Norman, like perhaps stand on an upright piano and punch him in the nose?

You betcha.

As I established earlier, George really isn't an ornery chap. He's never kicked a big dog in his entire life. But he is no longer content to stick even one more pin into his Norman doll. The hairy hand of frustration has now slapped George into a higher and faster gear.

To change the scene a bit, a mugger, known for his meanness, was finally arrested. Asked why he committed such unfriendly acts, he merely responded, "I want what *they* got."

Now then, does this imply that the have-nots are all ornery and the haves are angelic?

No. It doesn't. You and I know from personal experience that such is not the case. So here's a nifty experiment to help you create a villain for your fiction.

1. Make a list of people whom you know and dislike.
2. For each, also jot down a few *reasons* why you don't want this person as a companion. Be honest about it.

If you dislike Joe, is it because he's taller, more handsome, leaner, more athletic, brighter, better-paid?

What does Joe have in material goods that you covet?

Exactly what overt action has Joe taken against you? If, by chance, he's really never done *anything* mean to you, this enlightening fact will provide you with a wisp of insight into your own character, possibly leading you to one blushing conclusion:

You're the villain, not Joe.

To complete this exercise, you must do one thing more. Haul in a deep breath and then list as many admirable qualities in Joe's nature that you can muster the honesty and fortitude to set down.

One of the many facets of William Shakespeare's genius was that, when he wrote his plays, he put poetry in the mouth of a murderer.

He gave a daisy to Bathless Bart.

17
Gothic Ghost

Millicent is going mad, mad, mad.

Her madness is etched in facial horror, in full color, on the cover of any gothic novel. There she is, in a long period gown, dashing nocturnally away from a gloomy old castle perched atop a crag.

Who, you need not ask, is Millicent?

Needless to say, she is a pretty American girl who recently wed Sir Surly, more senior than she by at least a generation. His family (*old* money) is so wealthy that most of their dough is still in doubloons.

Is it fun being Mrs. Surly?

Well, perhaps at first it's a real kick. They met at a rushy 4-H Club party in Connecticut and, after *knowing* each other briefly, got hitched.

But, upon leaving America and arriving at Sir Surly's family manor, Gloomcrest, a forty-room pad overlooking a foggy Scottish moor, Millicent realizes that her life here could be a bowl of pits.

Did dear Sir (or Sur, as she dubs him) level with her about

his past? No, the cad did not. Somehow, to her, Sur now appears to be a mite more moody than he was back in carefree Connecticut.

Then cometh the sharpest barb. Does sweet Millicent the Innocent discover that she is not Sir Surly's first wife?

Is there a Great Hall at Gloomcrest, complete with a massive fireplace, over which hangs a giant portrait of the most beautiful, yet haunt-eyed, woman that Millie has ever seen?

Was she the first Mrs. Surly, now dead?

Golly gee, what a surprise!

However, innocent Millicent tries to be little wife perfecto. Sneakers wet from moor dew, she arranges a fresh clump of heather in an urn atop the harpsichord. Yet somebody moves it! (Not the piano, the urn.) Who would do such a deed and *why?*

None other than Mrs. Coldclam, who is Gloomcrest's housekeeper, tall and gaunt and dressed in black, with a personality damper than a Venetian dungeon. As she gazes respectfully upward at the portrait, she informs Millicent that "Mrs. Surly is allergic to heather."

Do we readers ever meet the first wife? No. Does she ever speak? Never. *But, oh boy, is she ever in the scene.*

Her ghost embeds itself in Millicent like ringworm.

Absence of heather was only the beginning. Seems like every Sunday evening, the kitchen crew whips up a gullion of sow's ear stew, which was the first Mrs. Surly's favorite snack. No amount of pleading by thoroughly modern Millie that they switch to Twinkies or Devil Dogs can alter the menu.

Millie awakens at midnight and reaches for Sur, only to find that his two-thirds of their bed is vacant and cold. Creeping down the great winding (and creaking) staircase, she discovers her hubby, alone, standing in the Great Hall, looking at the portrait.

Worse yet, Sur is barefoot on that icy marble floor; no longer does he wear the pink Playboy slippers that she'd given him, with the little bunnies on the toes.

Gone are other symbols of their early love . . . the Dolly

Parton bathmat, their new Jack-the-Ripper cutlery set, along with the leatherbound anthology she'd bought him, *Best of Screw*.

Yes, one by one, the tender souvenirs of romance erode, as Mrs. Coldclam tells how each would offend the first Mrs. Surly and her discriminating sow-ear taste.

Glowering at the portrait, Millie screams, "I hate you! I hate you! I *hate* you!" in a fit of pique and inspired dialogue.

Alone, she strolls on the moor, glancing back at Gloomcrest in the distance. Are there, Millie asks herself, other silent secrets buried inside those mossy and mildewed walls? Suddenly she sneezes.

Dang it! She's become allergic to heather.

Back at Gloomcrest, she commands Mrs. Coldclam to fetch her the Allerest. The housekeeper instead brings tea, smiles, and tells her that 'twas a hot swig of Oolong that offered Mrs. Surly (the first) fast, fast, fast relief.

Does the tea taste strange to Millicent?

You bet. Something got spiked into it and Millie bets it wasn't Allerest. Helplessly she slips into her lace nightie, her bed, and a coma.

As she slowly loses consciousness and flakes out from those harmful side effects, Millie hears music oozing up from the harpsichord. Had not Sur's first wife played it? Then she hears singing, a haunting melody that only a garroted ghost might gargle out. Too late, Millicent knows who warbles and why.

It is the ghostly and ghastly voice of the first Mrs. Surly, although long dead, belting the final chorus of her favorite loony tune:

"So Long, Oolong, How Long Ya Gonna Be Gone?"

Millicent knows now, just as the full-color cover of this novel promises, that she must flee the cozy comforts of Gloomcrest—even if it's dark outside and she is clad only in her official 4-H Club nightie.

In a trice, she splits.

"Come back, Millie!" yells Sur, following her astride Hoofrot, his black stallion.

"Never!" she cries.

"But I've forgotten all about . . . *her*. 'Tis you I crave, my dearest. *You!*"

He and Hoofrot overtake her.

Tall in the saddle, not to mention fantastic, Sur smiles down at her as the black stallion, lathery from exertion, snorts saliva onto the bib of her nightie. Yet, she asks, how can she trust the words of a man who rides a black horse and gnaws on a midnight snack of cold sow's ear?

However, she forgives him. They return to Gloomcrest and fall breathlessly into bed, enrapt in each others arms. How, she asks herself as she suddenly feels his gnarled hand toying with the hem of her 4-H Club nightie, will I ever teach an old dog a new trick?

"Tomorrow," Sur whispers, "the portrait shall be removed from the fireplace mantel of the Great Hall."

Hardly trusting herself to speak, she asks, "But where'll ya stash it, snooky?"

Sur slyly grins. "On the ceiling above our bed."

The young bride sighs. Victory at last. Beneath the musty quilts, the fingers of her left hand entwine with his. Her right hand, however, dives beneath her pillow to seek what she hopes is still there.

A half-eaten Twinkie.

As you can see, *anybody* can dash off a gothic novel. There's just one ingredient you must not omit.

Believe in ghosts.

Even if you plan to write a non-Gothic novel, you might still want to use a ghost in your story. I don't mean somebody in a sheet, falling over trunks in the attic or rattling a chain.

Seriously speaking, a ghost is someone who isn't around anymore. *Not necessarily dead.* Just departed.

You don't need to hang a portrait of Dear Departed over the massive fireplace. Or even ask your hero to carry a yellowing passport photo of D.D. in his wallet. The ghost is merely the presence of someone physically gone who affects the lives of those on the scene.

Are ghosts evil or good?

Either one. Earlier, in this chapter, the ghost of the first Mrs. Surly would hardly have been called just what the psychiatrist ordered. In a novel, someone now gone can still guide the hand and heart of a hero.

If you'd like an example, read the first chapter of *Fawn*. And the second chapter.

Fawn, a lad who is half white and half Mohawk, waits to kill his first deer. He waits silently, with patience, as Old Foot would have waited. For it was his grandfather who had made him his first arrow, his first bow, and had watched the boy grow strong enough to bend the wood, stretching the deergut bowstring until it touched his nose.

Throughout the novel, Fawn is guided by the wisdom of his grandfather. Yet, when Fawn sees war, he finally rejects Old Foot's song that war was joyful. War, decides Fawn, is a sad thing.

In the typical Gothic novel, the young heroine finally frees herself in the end from the grip of the ghost. In *Fawn*, a lad matures to carry with him the wisdom, but not the hatred, of a grandfather, Old Foot, he loved and admired.

Here is a ploy to charm a reader. More than that, to warm a reader's heart and possibly even your own:

When a young character in your novel recalls with respect the teachings of an older person, it produces a pleasantness, a reverence, an ingredient that all novels, in my opinion, should possess. Humankind is the only species on Earth, plant or animal, that invents religion, that is capable of sentiment, that *remembers*. We, apparently, all want to *believe* in something or someone greater than ourselves, to guide us, protect us, or whatever.

Sentiment can be saving old *things*.

Yet, as I see it and write it, the deepest and most worthy sentiment expresses itself in saving a thought, one that my grandmother or Fawn's grandfather gave us as a gift. If this makes any sense at all, the best sentiment is saving a sentiment. It is forever cherishing some little guideline given to us, as children, by someone older who loved us very much.

As this is true in my own memory of my father, mother, grandmother, and my teachers, I thereby conclude it to be a truth for my readers. And my characters.

I have only to examine the ghosts of my boyhood, again to hear the scoldings and the wisdom, and my heart is moved by memory. My parents were Plain People, quiet farmer folk who led almost silent lives. However, when they spoke, we youngsters listened up proper. Perhaps because Papa and Mama spoke only when their thinking deserved words.

You have only to read *A Day No Pigs Would Die* to know that my father's ghost will follow me forever. No, that's wrong. He will lead me. Haven Peck, like an honestly sweating Vermont plow, was worth following. His share still swims like quicksilver and knifes through a mud of trouble.

So I advise you, respect your past. Believe in your own sweet ghosts and your readers will believe in you.

18
The
Teacher

Oh, you'll do it.

Sooner or later, almost all emerging authors think about hunkering down at the old Underwood and knocking out a children's book. So, when your time comes to give it a gig, allow Peck to suggest that one of your characters in your book be a schoolteacher.

Why is using a teacher so natural?

The answer can be found in a simple examination of an adult's schedule. So much of one's adult life is spent at work, on the job. *A kid's job is school.* It is the work he does. School is a child's occupation. And, if he fails to work at his job, he fails (via report card) at home. Also among his peers.

The teacher is *the boss.*

In biology class, it is Miss Eggplant who must rule her roost and her roster. Woe betide little Filbert if he doesn't know Luther Burbank from Pliny the Elder.

However, even if your Miss Eggplant is hard-boiled, give her a soft center. The teacher who wins a reader is one who believes in cold facts and warm souls.

Consider your own childhood memories.

Is the teacher you fondly remember Mr. Backlash or Miss Doormat? Hardly. The teacher who cared enough to make you work, wash, and behave is that special person who will hold a hunk of your heart forever.

An excellent teacher I know once told me that she trains her kids as she would train a dog—with what she called her three As: Authority, Affection, and Approval.

I can conjure up no better advice for emerging writers. Those three A's can build a superb character. How?

Use touch.

A strong teacher character develops touch the way a mature football quarterback learns not to drill every pass like a frozen rope. A soft lob can be, in certain patterns, effective.

When a teacher stretches out a hand, with a hanky, to wipe a few flecks of mud from the face of a dirty little boy, a reader also has to be touched. Words like *care* or *love* or *tenderness* are so unnecessary to caption such a picture. Avoid them!

It is the physical exchange that really grabs us. The laying on of hands, to heal. It's touch.

But the touching also can be intellectual as well as physical. To wit:

I happen to know a very funny man, a retired teacher, whose name is Mervis Tittle.

My sides nearly split when Mervis claimed that he was the only high school football coach who never became a principal. Actually, he was an English teacher. They made him coach the football team because his name was Tittle. At the time, Y.A. Tittle was the revered quarterback hero of the New York Giants.

Mervis Tittle would make a nifty character in a book. He was a small man, rather thin, who had never played football at all. Mr. Tittle knew about split infinitives—to quickly tell the story—not split ends.

I'm not going to write a football book about Mervis, so perhaps you can.

He deserves one. Because no 138-pound English teacher ever trained harder, bought more books on football, or stayed up later trying to decipher the difference between a trap block and a blitz.

I have met several of the boys (now men) who played for Coach Tittle. They talk about him as if he were a combination of Bear Bryant and Amos Alonzo Stagg.

He couldn't pass or punt.

Instead, he read poetry to them, poems about average men who were somehow capable of performing one heroic act. About a boy at sea who stood on a burning deck.

I've watched grown men cry when they talk about him. Not because he was, or ever pretended to be, a great coach. He was far more . . . a great gentleman.

If you visit the Football Hall of Fame in Canton, Ohio, you'll see no bronze statue of Mervis Tittle. His teams lost almost every game. Still, his boys carried him off the field, after every final whistle, because they felt that Coach Tittle was bigger than victory, or defeat. Even if they repeatedly lost, he taught them to be winners.

Notice anything?

Have you noticed how I have rambled on and on and *on* about Mervis Tittle? I do so with a purpose.

Why? Because he is a *character.* He is unique. One of a kind. Smaller than guards or tackles yet bigger than life. Men and women like Mr. Tittle are builders.

People such as he build your book.

It takes only one puny Mervis Tittle to anchor a novel. Because your readers who read about him, like the boys who played for him, will know that there's not one ounce of *quit* in his 138 pounds.

"I shall never ask you lads to win," he once told them in a locker room prior to a game. "But I shall be so very disappointed if even one of you fails to play his finest."

Numbers on a stadium scoreboard cannot measure a man who stood so short, yet so tall. Good writing is not like TV, a quantitative medium. It is, instead, the *quality of character*, more than any other ingredient, that polishes your work.

In later years, Mr. Tittle was replaced, as a new and younger coach was hired. Mr. Tittle then was free to teach English and read aloud the poems he loved. However, his story, as he told it to me, has a rather dramatic finish.

Finally, the team won a football game, beating a tough rival. The players dashed into the stands to lift Mr. Tittle high upon their shoulders.

"Hey!" a fan yelled up to him. "You must be their coach."

"No," said Mr. Tittle, "I'm their English teacher."

Again, allow me to say this to you please:

Get carried away!

I just did, in writing my anecdote about Mr. Mervis Tittle. Why did I do it? Because I couldn't help myself. Couldn't stop. I can't resist writing about the countless fascinating people who have so enriched my life. In my books I do it all the time. And, if fat royalty checks are any proof to you, my readers can't stop reading about them.

So here's my advice. If you write a book for young readers, at least consider a *teacher* as one of your major or minor characters.

My twenty-ninth book is entitled *Banjo*.

In it, there's a teacher named Miss Crowder who holds a football in her hands and yells out a cheer to her students. Is the cheer about football? Hardly. It's about a *theme* that she is asking her class to write.

You'll read more about *Banjo* in the chapter entitled "Short Story Now . . . Book Later."

Now then, here comes a question that you may already be asking. Is a teacher a character only in books for children?

No.

Good Morning, Miss Dove is a novel about a teacher in a small town. I won't tell you about it here, because in limited space, I couldn't do justice to such a superbly written book. A telephone call to your public library will inform you whether or not it's there for you to read, if you're at all interested.

My point is that teachers are people.

Once in a while, I teach a course in creative writing at a college. But I've never really been a teacher, week in and year out, decade upon decade, in a public or private school.

However, as grist for an adult novel, I believe that a teacher could make an intriguing hero or heroine. Why? Because a teacher exists in *two* separate worlds. One, a world of young pupils. Two, the private life among adults.

First off, dealing with kids would be fascinating. And frustrating. Then, at quitting time, the teacher limps home, drained of patience and with nerves aflutter, perhaps to an equally trying environment of family-life problems.

You, no doubt, have heard a recent expression: teacher burnout.

Can't you see how a teacher could fall victim to such a condition? I surely can. Inside, the spring of human tension winds tighter and tighter. The pressure gauge of self-control begins to point its warning arrow into the red area of potential explosion.

Job security, or rather *job insecurity*, is possibly the ring that could pull the pin of a teacher's grenade.

Especially now, today, when the growth of private schools seems to indicate that there will soon be as many private schools in America as there will be public ones. How does this affect your character (your teacher)?

Is he now less interested in education and more concerned with just plain animal survival?

Earlier, we said that a teacher exists in *two* worlds: classroom and home. But that's inadequate. There is a third element in a teacher's life. Administration. A teacher has to contend with a department head, a principal, a superintendent, the school board, the taxpayers—plus the growing armies of county, state, and federal overseers.

All of these groups can supply your novel with *characters*.

Problem: You (if you're not a teacher) possibly don't know

what all of these types of administrators are like. What do you do?

Here's what you *don't* do. You, the writer, don't fake it. Here is what you *can* do. Be honest. Contact a teacher and explain that you're writing a novel about a teacher.

But will the teacher you wish to interview help you?

Not all will volunteer. So search until you find one brave enough to let off steam from the pressure gauge. Let you peek inside the grenade.

My guess is *yes*, you'll locate a teacher who will open up, one who'll be almost eager to inform you of the pitfalls, or pits, of the job. People like to talk. So listen up. Take notes.

Warning! If you stumble onto a *griper*, let the teacher spew out venom and "expel" it for an hour or two. Then, guide the conversation around to more positive and happier aspects of the job.

"Are there moments," you ask, "when, in spite of all the headaches, it's worthwhile?"

Ask about the one special pupil in that teacher's life who is a rainbow beyond a storm of aggravation. There will be at least one. In the life of every teacher, bar none, there are those exceptional little candles that can brighten a classroom into a birthday cake.

After all, Miss Kelly had Soup and me.

19
The
Nobody Kid

Want to know if an idea is lousy?

Here's what we do these days to determine the answer. We somehow want to try it out in our schools on kids.

Although I shall never understand why, problems that should be comprehended (or ignored) by adults, are saddled to the backs and brains of our young for children to test or to endure.

From viewing existing social patterns, it seems obvious to me that American adults, regardless of color, are not too anxious to integrate. However, some federal judge is bound to say, "Let's make the *kids* test it."

Needless to say, integration will come skipping along whenever Mother Nature is good and ready. But not until. And every bus on Earth will do little or naught to goose the old girl to a higher gear.

Issues fascinate me.

If you intend to warp yourself into a writer, issues should also fascinate you. Why? Because *issues*, especially burning, controversial ones, have a way of heating up characters. They're gold mines.

Let's handle a hot one. But remember, the core of this chapter is this: The issue is not seen through *our* eyes, but through the eyes and ears and heart of a child.

We've decided to write a novel about an issue in our community, one that raises every temperature and tattles every tongue in town.

The issue is *creation versus evolution*.

Every mouth is yapping and foaming. Whatever they lack in reason, they make up with emotion. Tempers flare. It's a battle royal between the ministers and the scientists. Everyone is cocksure he's totally right and the other guys are dead wrong.

Sooner or later, a nincompoop will come up with the inspired suggestion that, if we need a battleground for a battle, the *school* is the only logical place. After all, we can't have *adults* getting wounded.

So, like war, we send *our boys, and girls,* to slaughter.

The adults are mad with joy. Because their buns are going to be blessing the bench, on the sidelines, watching the plasma pelt the playground. A ref tweets a whistle and the game is all go. On one side of the field they wave Bibles. The other side waves white mice.

Somewhere, out on the fifty yard line, stands one very confused little boy.

Georgie doesn't want to play.

All he knows is that the adults suited him in black, told him that the name of his team is the Gospel Thumpers; and ordered him, at the age of nine, to get in there, mix it up, and be a man.

His best pal, Willie, is on the other team, the White Mice. Georgie hangs around with Willie and they have a lot of fun collecting bottle caps. He can't understand why his parents are now telling him that Willie's parents are evil people who don't deserve to live with decent folk.

Willie's parents say the same about Georgie's.

It's a bore. Georgie remembers the good old days when Dad used to take him fishing and Mom was a den mother for the Cub troop. All his parents do now is go to meetings. Georgie is forced to go too. There's a ton of talk and even more temper, which spurs Georgie to ask the only important question:

"Can we go home now?"

Home, as Georgie sees it, isn't nearly as much fun as it used to be. There are always too many leaflets. No supper. Mom's busy folding and Dad's licking the envelopes.

Georgie wants to scoot next door and trade bottle caps with Willie. He announces his plans, but is quickly told by his loving mother to "stay away from those people."

At school, there's Mrs. Bancroft, who Georgie knows is the best teacher in the whole world. She wore a pith helmet on her head when they were learning all about a place called The Congo. But after the day they had cupcakes at school, during which Mrs. Bancroft had said a prayer, Mrs. Bancroft's eyes looked red.

Willie told Georgie that he'd seen Mrs. Bancroft reading a letter and that she was going to lose her job or maybe go to jail.

Mrs. Bancroft's husband, Fred, doesn't sing in the choir at church anymore. Georgie doesn't understand why. His parents tell him that it isn't Mrs. Bancroft who's in trouble. Instead, it's Mr. Wheeler, the science teacher, over at the high school.

Georgie remembers the day that Mrs. Bancroft invited Mr. Wheeler to visit their class. He brought mice and talked about evolution, which, Georgie thought, meant that people shouldn't dump a soda can or trash a road.

He's not allowed to walk to school with Willie.

A leaflet comes in the mail. Georgie's father rips it up and kicks the piano because the leaflet says that God created white mice as well as Adam and Eve.

Georgie recalls that Adam and Eve are the names of the two mice that belong to Mr. Wheeler, the science teacher.

Willie says that his big sister's friend, Alice, saw the mice *breeding* in a cage at the high school, and that's why Mr. Wheeler is going to get fired. Because he has a dirty brain.

Sunday morning arrives.

The service is very short because their preacher, Reverend Bailey, is in the hospital. Somebody beat him up. Georgie can't believe it, because Reverend Bailey is a good guy who smiles a lot and used to be a champion baseball player.

At home, instead of seeing Willie on Sunday afternoon, Georgie has to help Mom stuff more envelopes. They have to mail out a flyer. Georgie reads some of it, which is all about Adam and Eve. He doesn't know why Mom wants to tell folks about Mr. Wheeler's pets.

Eve is going to have baby mice.

Georgie hears this from Willie's sister. But when he tells Mom and Dad, he gets sent from the supper table to his room.

It's dark. Georgie can't sleep.

Downstairs, his parents are talking about Reverend Bailey, who said that mice were God's creatures and who didn't hit back when he'd gotten beat up. Dad was saying that another minister in town said that Adam and Eve were only two leaves on the tree of time. And if a human began as one cell, the cell was God's idea, and it wasn't invented by some scientist.

Then he heard more. Mr. Wheeler doesn't go to their church, but he had the nerve to visit the Reverend Bailey in the hospital; and if things like that went on, what is this town coming to?

The saddest part was next day, when a kid in school asks Mrs. Bancroft if it's true . . . Did somebody break into the school and kill the mice? Hesitantly, she admits to them it is true.

"Was it a cat?" Georgie asks.

No.

They even killed Eve's little babies.

Georgie tells Mrs. Bancroft, "Maybe we could all say a prayer for the baby mice so they'd go to Heaven." There is no prayer. Mrs. Bancroft hugs Georgie, very softly, telling him that he's not the only one who doesn't understand.

A novel can be written.

But when you write about an issue, please take one very important hunk of advice from your pal Peck. Be sure that people on *both sides* of the issue have intelligence and sensitivity, as

(115)

well as emotion. If you have an ax to grind and you're too personally overwrought, you'll probably write *Angels vs. Apes*, and none of your novel will ring real.

Balance your book! Don't let it be the pretties against the uglies. Let your pure little Georgie see the good in the people of both parties. He likes them, yet cannot savvy why good folks are somehow hurting each other.

The entire story can be told by Georgie, *from his point of view;* as he sees, hears, feels his school and his church and his town go sour. Mice, bottle caps, and a best pal are no longer in his life.

A little nobody kid can be somebody.

Characters pop up from issues. Like weeds.

In your community, your school, and possibly even in your home, issues detonate constantly. You may not believe this, but every one of those issues has two sides. That's good! Because if all of you are on the same side, there is *no issue* at all. No opponents and no clash of characters.

Please don't tell me that you have tripped gaily through life's meadow of larks and daisies and never heard an argument. I won't buy it. So, at the next spat you overhear, move in. Take notes. If the fight is taking place at Bruto's Bar & Grill, perhaps you might want to click on your tape recorder, just prior to getting your nose busted.

The reason that I entitled this chapter "The Nobody Kid" is this: We, as adults, have long lost our childlike purity. The sweet little candle of virginity has been snuffed out by a hairy paw. The adult hero in your novel, Harry Paw, can no longer see both sides of the issue.

Harry sees *his* side.

But he may have a young son or daughter who has a friend in what Daddy calls "the enemy camp."

What adds to the drama of your characterization of everyone involved is this: Nobody listens to the Nobody Kid. After all, he's just a kid, so what does *he* know?

In your novel, the kid is your *bridge.*

(116)

His purity spans the deep chasm of discontent, straining and stretching to join, or to rejoin, the two groups of adults that are now divided.

Now for a key element. Possibly the crux of your story is not how the principal issue is fought or resolved. The key to the entire book is . . . *what happens to the kid.*

Is he, like a bridge, being yanked physically and spiritually by both sides? Is the *issue* tearing him apart? Probably not. What rips his little heart in twain is when he realizes what's happening to good people on both sides. It is possible that he is almost entirely unaware of the issue. To him, the issue doesn't really matter. But the people he knows, and loves, matter very much.

As a reader reads your story, what is *his* reaction?

Does the reader care who wins in the town, the Bible Thumpers or the White Mice? Oh, he might care a fig. Yet what the reader really wants to learn, as he reads, is this:

What's going to happen to the child?

Were I to write a book like this, I believe I'd have the youngster tell the entire story, from his child's point of view. Whether the style is first person or third person is unimportant. Here is the nut of your structure:

Put a cherub in Hell.

Warning: the child does not have to be a perfect little angel, the way you and I were when *we* were that age, faultless in every way. Smear some mud on the angel's face and on his actions. Get him dirty.

If you live in a childless home and you can honestly confess you're not completely sure of what children are like, march yourself (if you have a strong stomach) to the nearest playground or schoolyard. Five minutes of observation will suffice. Then, as you go shrieking homeward in horror, you'll be an expert.

By the way, I wrote a novel, a rather successful one, on this format . . . a cool youth in the middle of a hot issue. Its title is *Justice Lion.* The issue is Prohibition; the arena, a court of law;

the hero, a lad in his middle teens. His name is Muncie Bolt.

Is he torn?

Well, his father is the prosecuting attorney, but the defendant is the father of his closest pal. So, he is torn indeed. For he is also in love with the defendant's daughter. And he respects his father.

As far as you're concerned, right now, it shouldn't matter much to you how *Justice Lion* turns out in the end. What's important to you is this: I've merely illustrated one structure, one plot, one issue, one situation, in which young Muncie Bolt plays both the *bridge* and the *camera* that films the action.

So, that's the way to do it, my friend. Think of a burning issue in a community. Then tell your story through the camera eyes of one youthful observer, one whose heart becomes gradually involved.

He is the Nobody Kid, the story's essence and its soul.

20
The
Show-Off

It's my very favorite sport.

To be honest, to tell you the straight of it, I would rather *show off* in front of somebody than do anything else. Perhaps that's why I learned how to spin a rope or play ragtime piano or ski. I'm smart enough to know it's why I played football.

Even now, I flex at the beach.

Showing off is why I make speeches; and, if asked, a sermon. I adore it. Give me an audience and I'm a hawg in mud. At the club, when pretty girls are watching us macho males at tennis, I hit the ball a ton.

Happiness is knowing who you are. Also what you are. Spectators turn me on.

I am the incurable ham.

There is no cure; and were a pill invented, or shots, I wouldn't take any.

Secretly, I've always been a bit suspicious of the introverts who never show off. This is only fair. The reserved army can be rather vocal in their criticism of hotdoggers like me. Maybe the folks who never *flaunt* it ain't *got* it.

Show-offs make nifty characters.

Why? Because it's so *human* to yell, "Hey, everybody . . . look at *me!* I'm finally dancing the Charleston."

Any trait, regardless of whether it's admirable, is useful to a writer. For this is how we all behave. We're mixtures. Therefore, if you're about to cast your characters for a novel, don't forget Kate who wants to tap dance in church during Bach's B-Minor Mass.

Kiss me, Kate. I love you.

And if you can tap dance, yodel, and spin a rope all at the same time, we're leaving you in the act.

No sooner do you establish Kate and her troika of talents, than along comes Edith, sitting in the front pew with her spine more rigid than a West Point brace.

Edith does not approve of Kate, her taps, her yodel, her looping rope that just bulldogged the choir director, and all that makeup that Kate trowels onto her ruby lips. In fact, Edith now elbows Ralph, her husband, whose bored head has nodded, escaping Bach.

"Look at that hussy show off," she hisses.

Ralph stares; and then smiles, as Kate is wearing scanty skirt, spangled tights, and tassels. His foot begins to tap, like Kate's. He's *into* it.

Up he jumps, also dancing.

It's not easy to Shuffle Off to Bach, but Kate and Ralph are doing a hat-and-cane number you wouldn't believe.

It's too much for the choir master, Mr. Prawltriller. So he starts doing a number on Ralph and whales him with a baton. One by one, the choir stops singing Bach and cleverly modulates into something more modern, one of the hits by The Drooling Stones.

One show-off, Kate, started it.

You *can* have your Kate and Edith too. All you start with is one extrovert.

As I told you earlier in this chapter, show-offs make useful characters in your novel. They're nifty folks for fiction.

Books are written scene by scene.

Therefore, picture your particular show-off in the center of a room at a party. What's he doing? Card tricks. Even though it happens to be midnight on New Year's Eve and everyone at the party is kissing, he fans a deck and insists, "Take a card. Any card."

Picture him as the hub.

For some reason, he has finally attracted everyone's attention (perhaps by standing naked on the piano and hollering).

What's useful is the *reaction* to the show-off, as useful as the S.O. is himself. Do people laugh at him? Ignore him? Pity him? Push him off the piano and punch his nose? Is there someone in the room at the party who secretly wishes that *he* could do card tricks?

Be sure to explain—to yourself, before you even attempt to write page one—*why* the extrovert shows off. Human behavior, like animal behavior, always harbors some logical reason. This you must establish before you write. It may or may not be necessary to explain it to your readers.

But if it *is* necessary, don't give us *your* explanation. Show it, by the use of an earlier scene—say, earlier that day, when the boss strides into S.O.'s office and fires him.

The urge to be and feel significant is a very normal hunger within all of us. Even we lemons crave limelight. We wear purple sox, or no sox, and we wear T-shirts that shout messages to the world that we want to belong to a yet-unformed club, some little society of nobodies that wants the fifth face on Mount Rushmore to be that of Don Knotts.

We bumpersticker our cars.

For a cause, we wear a button on a lapel that screams to the world what we stand for, want, or hate. Worse yet, we carry other campaign buttons with us and try to pin them on our friends. Even on the lapels of people we've barely met.

Oh, how we want to *impress* somebody.

If you don't believe that, read your latest memo. One that you composed. In it are words you don't normally use at home.

They are show-off words. Long wordy words, where a short, crisp word would have been clearer.

So, you see, all show-offs do not wear lampshades on their heads at parties. Beg, or bug, the piano player to play "Melancholy Baby."

Within all of us lurks an S.O. waiting with a card trick, a lampshade, or a pin for somebody's lapel. The tragedy is that some of us don't realize how comical we are.

However, not all show-offs are comic.

Some are sad. There is Victor, who has never been victorious at anything. At dinner parties, Victor builds a pyramid using the host's crystal, and then threatens to rip away the tablecloth without tumbling a tumbler.

Vic tells jokes that aren't funny.

Dialect is not one of his talents, so Pat and Mike sound as though they were hatched in Yokohama or Rochester.

Paula is Vic's wife.

She still loves him because she knows Victor as well as she knows herself. She's aware that inside Vic there's a little boy who never quite grew up, and he's screaming, "Please notice me!"

Nobody, you see, ever yelled "Great shot, Vic!" at a basketball game. At the office he was never given authority, a title, or a rug.

Vic wears neckties that glow in the dark and read, "Kiss me, I'm Irish." In the Saint Patrick's Day parade he tries so hard to march in step. He always volunteers to carry the banner. No one else wants to.

Paula and Victor have no children.

Vic's brother, Clarence, has six sons. At the birth of each nephew, Vic hopes that his brother will name the new boy Victor. It never happens.

The parlor tricks, Saint Paddy's banner, the glowing neckties are not what Vic really wants. He longs to be good at something. In the past, he has sent away for a mail-order course in karate, a pamphlet on how to raise fighting cocks, and magic kits.

At a community meeting, he'd give anything if a neighbor would ask, "What do you think we ought to do, Victor?" No one does. Vic gets up and tells them anyhow. But nobody listens, which causes him to shout a lot.

Victor dislikes parties where teams are chosen, in front of everyone. He knows he'll be last to get picked. If caught in such a social situation, he'll insist, "Hey! I wanna be a captain."

He never is.

In his lapel there's a fake flower that can squirt a curious face with water whenever Vic squeezes the bulb in his pocket. "Smell my flower," he says. No one's nosy.

Nobody except Paula. At more than one party she's taken a facial splashing, and the wetness she wipes from her face is not all water. Some of the drops are genuine grief. She has to sacrifice her own face to save his.

Many a show-off is a guffawing clown whose pain and antics mask his torment.

Who knows? Perhaps I am one of them.

21
Tuba
and Violins

I've decided to form an orchestra.

So we don't disturb the neighbors, I figure a nifty place to rehearse will be downstairs in our cellar. As I have only twenty folding chairs, which I got really cheap from a retired funeral director, we'll have twenty musicians.

Nineteen bass drums and a silent dog whistle.

Absurd? Quite.

My orchestra will, no doubt, be boomed to failure because of its lack of variety. And that can also be the reason a novel fails.

There's a movie I want you to see.

Its title is *Friendly Persuasion* and it stars a friend of mine. (We attended Rollins College together in the good old days when the school wasn't trying to produce great scholars. It produced great kids.) His name is one you know, Anthony Perkins.

The film has a beautiful theme song, "Thee I Love."

This movie is about the Civil War and a very quiet Quaker family, violin people, who are fortunate to have a very loud lady, played by Marjorie Main, as a neighbor. She was a gifted character actress, perhaps best known for her portrayal of Ma Kettle.

In *Friendly Persuasion*, she is a refreshing tuba among violins. Delightful contrast.

I inserted a tuba, the Widow Starr, into my historical novel, *Hang for Treason*. To me, such a contrast works in movies and in books.

Needless to say, you're going to run into a tizzy of trouble if you try reversing the ratio. In other words, among a dinny den of tubas, one violin will be virtually lost.

In *Justice Lion*, I did it again.

This novel takes place in 1923 in a quiet Vermont town called Liberty. The book's key family is composed of only two people, a soft-spoken lawyer, Jesse Bolt, and his teenage son, Muncie.

Petunia Bly is their cleaning lady, their neighbor, and a caring friend. She wants not only to mother her own brood of countless children, but also to be a mother to the entire town. Come mealtime, there's always room at her tumultuous table for at least one more platoon of Russian infantry.

There's an old Vermont expression, usually spoken about too-loud people: "Empty wagons rattle the most."

Petunia Bly, however, is far from stupid. She's bright, witty, sensitive, aware of other people's pain even more than her own. She's big, motherly, and warm as a morning pillow. We hear depth from her tuba.

Not all tubas will play so pleasantly. There's another kind of loud lip that, in an entirely opposite way, will serve to add variety to your cast. The Crashing Bore.

Some jokester once defined a Crashing Bore as follows: A man who was born in Texas, served in the Marines, and then went to Notre Dame.

Every jest sprouts a sprig of truth.

Above and beyond all other characteristics, the Crashing Bore is usually singular in dimension.

He's the dentist, who, even at cocktail parties, seems to be constantly examining everyone's overbite.

Or he is the psychologist who doesn't converse with you. He *probes*. As he leers behind his thick lenses, you realize that he suspects you hate your mother. Because *his* mother hated *him*.

There's the chap who owns the local bootery, and he's staring at everyone's shoes. The party is black-tie and you're suddenly sorry you wore your yellow Keds.

Tuba versus violin can also be manifested by two characters, one of whom is tender, the other tough. One is a beardless youth; his companion, a grizzled grandfather. It works. Violets growing in the low shade next to the rotting stump of a former massive tulip tree.

As owls and pussycats foil for one another, experience and innocence do likewise, pulling well together under one dramatic yoke.

Sometimes it works better when you establish a two-generation gap. Grandma and granddaughter. Gramps and grandson. Mother and daughter, as well as father and son, blend less smoothly. Kids and parents seem too often to snap at each other's throats. But we tend to adore, and spoil, all our grandchildren, because it is so natural to aid the enemies of our enemies.

Kirk's Law sets forth such a unity.

It begins with father-and-son friction. They don't get along at all. Like all people, they quarrel. *Friction* is folks. Dad is taking Sonny up north, from Connecticut, in order to dump him with an elderly gentleman, a wilderness guide, whose name is Sabbath Kirk.

Mr. Kirk and the boy, Collin, clash respectively as experienced tuba and innocent violin. Brass and string. *Contrast*.

I made a related point in the first textbook I wrote, *Secrets of Successful Fiction*, warning emerging writers not to tumble into what I label the Tweedledee-Tweedledum pitfall. In brief, what creates a dramatic situation is not sameness. People who have a lot in common usually wind up boring one another—in real life as well as in novels.

(126)

Stan Laurel and Sherlock Holmes were violins. Oliver Hardy and Doctor Watson were tubas. Thus, as you cast your story, the process is somewhat similar to adjusting your TV set.

Fiddle with a contrast button.

It'll sharpen your personality picture. Enhance the lights and darks. Deepen the shadows and let the highlights sparkle in sunshine. A French tuba and a Huron violin.

One of the many tricks that successful novelists use, when building the cast of characters for a piece of fiction, is this:

They create two people who somehow do not really belong together, yet form a bond. I can think of no better example than George and Lenny in John Steinbeck's superb novel, *Of Mice and Men.*

George is puny and wise, while Lenny is massive and simpleminded. Together they survive in a hostile world. To oversimplify, Lenny is the tuba; George, the violin.

Think of your cast as a variety show.

The basis for romantic comedy in *The Owl and the Pussycat* is the love that is discovered between the owlish professor and a painted lady. One is an intellectual; the other, a treadworn floozie.

There is an aspect of such a union, subtle though it may be, that touches our hearts. It is this: Someone finds room in his heart to appreciate human value in a person who is not at all like himself. It's too easy to approve of those who think, dress, and worship as we do.

Anyone can love a clean baby.

It takes far more bowels to love, and to tend thoroughly, a soiled one. Yet this is the measure, is it not, of our mature responsibility?

Variety is contrast. Strips of chrome on a black limousine. Somehow, to think visually even further, the human eye is fascinated by extreme black and white. Scotch, a skunk, zebras, nuns, and newspapers.

Ergo, so much of character contrast is visual variety. The physically lean bodies of Laurel and Holmes versus the portly personages of Hardy and Watson.

Another contrast, far more subtle, is having a young (or culturally deprived) character as the protagonist who is on hand to describe to readers a complicated event.

For example, *Justice Lion* is a courtroom novel.

The book is written entirely in the first person, which means that the case, though complicated in court by lawyers and judges, is simplified through the eyes of young Muncie Bolt. An adult situation distilled by a youthful mind to its most rudimentary values.

In *The King's Iron*, one sub-major character is a Huron warrior, Blue Goose. A Jesuit tells him that he must no longer be a savage but must become a Catholic, in order to see God. The Huron does not believe this to be true.

I have only, he thinks, to look at the color of a sundown sky to know that God sees Blue Goose.

Contrast. A black-robed Jesuit and an almost naked Huron warrior. Their faiths as varying as much as their feathers. Two men, neither of whom is intellectually or socially capable of understanding the other.

Here are a few guidelines for you, to assist your creating a George and a Lenny, a majestic duo of opposites.

1. One is rich. The other is poor.
2. One is a city, the other, a country, character.
3. One is old; the other, young.
4. One is formally educated, bookish, and speaks in high-toned language. The other is uneducated but wise in human understanding.
5. One is a loud extrovert, while his companion (perhaps the one who tells the story) is silently reflective.
6. One is totally honest, yet outwardly poor. The other is a con artist, a fast talker who somehow discovers that what he himself lacks and yearns for is exactly what the poor man holds in his heart.
7. One has social clout, possibly due to military or business rank. The other is a private or a janitor.

Needless to say, the most obvious juxtaposition of opposites is simply *a man and a woman*. No one has ever begun to understand this relationship, and no one ever shall. Yet most of us are in awe of its mystery, its charm, its bliss and battling and bills.

Opposites attract? Possibly, but they also *attack*. And from this confrontation eventually can sprout a warmth of mutual understanding that can hum a heartstring.

Tubas and violins, although different in so many respects, can play the same tune.

22
It's
Party Time

Why do people throw parties?

Because there's nothing quite like a cocktail party to bring out the *worst* in everybody.

There's one act I always perform at parties, particularly if there's (1) no piano, (2) no leggy blonde with a tan, or (3) no big comfortable chair to flake out in.

I corner a liberal and torture it.

However, feeling a mite contrite about such an unfair practice, I have amended my favorite ploy. I won't do that anymore. From now on, I'll corner *three* liberals. So, intellectually speaking, the sides will be even.

If there's a piano, I torture everybody.

There's only one thing worse than a cocktail party. Driving home after it's over.

You know what *that's* like, don't you?

At the door, you've had your hat and coat on for twenty minutes. Your hand is jingling the car keys because your wife is still talking to the hostess, who is also talking.

At last you start the car.

Absolutely nothing is said. No word spoken for at least two hundred miles. Finally, your wife cracks the rotten egg of silence.

"Well, I *hope* you're happy, Ralph.'

"Me? What did I do?"

"You know very well what you did. And it will certainly be a surprise to me if we're *ever* invited to the Hendersons' again."

"I didn't do a thing."

"Except for singing that *song*."

"What song?"

"You know perfectly well. That *army* song. And when you used that *word*, you should have *seen* Irma Filmore's face."

"I've already seen Irma's face. What's more, I play golf with Chuck Filmore, and I'll wager that Irma hears that word rather often."

So it goes.

Thus, if you want to be a writer, party it up. Gather ye rosebuds. And thorns. Not that every book demands a party. Yet such a gathering invites dialogue and brings out the eccentricities of character personality like a tray of appetizers.

Humans are like tinder sticks.

Rub a couple together and you'll start a fire. Sparks will fly. A married couple at a party can be flint and steel . . . heated even further, of course, when Ralph stands on the piano with a lampshade on his head.

To make matters worse, he has just returned from a trip to the powder room and is not completely reassembled.

People skip around a lot at parties. They circulate. But I don't want you to do it. Stay put. Record your party through the eyes and ears of one person, one camera, in the head of Ralph's wife, Gladice.

It sort of has to be Gladice.

Why? Because old Ralph's been into the Red Eye (or vice-versa) and is having too much fun to be aware of anything. He's so into the party that he's out of it. His whistle isn't wet. It's drowning.

This affair at the Hendersons' means a lot to Gladice. That's because Muriel Henderson is president of Garden Club; or maybe PEO, a sorority, of which Gladice is a new member.

Now then, let's pull a switch.

The party is *not* at the Hendersons'. It's a weekday morning brunch, at Gladice's, and all her PEO sisters are coming to swap secrets. Gladice is the Guard. Ralph kids her, asking her, "Who plays tackle?"

For the past thirty-six hours, Gladice has been buffing her house, until even the cat reeks of Lemon Pledge.

But, now the morning has dawned, there's a major problem. Ralph is sick. Instead of going to the office he lingers at home. The PEO ladies are streaming to the door as Gladice spots Ralph, who has employed neither comb nor razor, parading through the parlor in a bathrobe the Salvation Army would reject.

Gladice is sweating as Ban fails.

She must act! Can she shut Ralph into the garage with the cat? As the doorbell rings, Ralph asks Gladice if she's seen that manila folder that he took out of his briefcase last night.

In marches PEO, in step.

Gladice gushes all over everyone, then pirouettes to her kitchen to inspire a reluctant Mr. Coffee, while Irma Filmore inspects for dust. Muriel Henderson resists straightening a tilted picture.

Something is on the blink, Gladice notices, with Mr. Coffee. He's cold and so unfeeling. That's because Ralph has unplugged him to work the toaster. But that's when good old Ralph rides to the rescue like the cavalry.

"Want me to play the piano?" he asks.

No jury, Gladice is now thinking, would convict her. From the refrigerator, she pulls out that special coffee cake, the recipe for which came directly from *Joy of Marriage*. A piece is missing, torn away by Gladice knows who.

Ralph sneezes.

Then he asks Gladice where the Contac is. He says he'll settle for aspirin, but the bottle's empty. So he announces that maybe one of the PEO ladies has some aspirin in her purse. Gladice doesn't hear. She's too busy remortaring the coffee cake.

You see? Fiction *is* folks. You can talk about a party until all the ashtrays spill over, but it comes to life only when *folks* are involved and Mr. Coffee is revolting. So is Ralph.

The party is not important. But in the mind of Gladice Glutz, it is crucial because it's now, today, and *hers*.

A book, as I see it, is a party.

You, the author, invite people you like and a few you loathe because you have to have Irma's white glove seeking a wisp of lint that will make her day—and ruin Gladice's.

Remember this. No book, and no party, comes off without a hitch. If nothing foul takes place in your fiction, you may be able to portray the human condition as naught but candlelight and gypsy violins, all peachy poo . . . and if you do, it's dull.

So invite Ralph and Irma.

Plop a hockey puck into the punch. Let dear Irma Filmore discover the dust. And be sure that Ralph in his bathrobe is there, letting the cat out of the bag (or the garage) because Gladice forgot to warn him of Muriel's allergy.

In fiction, the scene cannot go quietly unmolested. You, the author, have to *disrupt*. Only then does your scene become comic, or dramatic.

Such a scene may add silver to Gladice's hair, but it adds gold to your pocket.

Speaking of pocketbooks, as Gladice's party grinds on, Ralph, now desperate for medication of any variety, is quietly searching through all of the purses for aspirin. Being thoughtful, he doesn't want to interrupt the ritual.

Until he finally drops Irma's bag.

A small glass vial of perfume, Torrid Nuit, smashes on the hall's tile floor, flooding the festivity with fragrance. Ralph cuts his bare foot on the glass and screams to Gladice for a Band-Aid. There aren't any, he discovers, in the bathroom cabinet's little tin box.

Like aspirin, they have gone. And right about now, Gladice is considering going, too. Forever.

The emancipated cat has crept softly into the meeting, on little cat feet, and has selected a lap to jump up into . . . Muriel's. Dander dances merrily upward into her sinus cavities.

So, dear writer, throw a party. Characters will come and also come alive. But you'll strike out unless disaster strikes in. You'll be wise indeed to invite one pivotal guest.

Invite Trouble.

23
Animal Talk

Fiction is folks.

If you're as much of a patsy for pets as Peck is, you might feel that animals are folks too. And they reveal the depths of character of the people who surround them.

My father, Haven Peck, once told me this: "It matters not what a man's religion is unless his dog and cat are the better for it."

As a writer, I believe that a professional way to show a character in a book is to allow the reader a look at, for example, a farmer tending his stock. It's my guess that a great deal of the success of my first novel, *A Day No Pigs Would Die*, stems from its intimate human-animal contact.

If you wish to create a boring character, here's the ploy. Depict your guy, or gal, thinking or caring or doing *only* for himself, or herself.

Such pitfalls are easy to avoid.

All you have to do is show a person, tired from work, pausing to stoop and lift a bug out of a puddle.

That's all, just a bug.

Please note that the tended animal does not have to be epic in importance. It doesn't have to be General Washington's white horse or Lassie. A bug will surely serve. Perhaps the more lowly and more helpless, the better. A kitten will do.

Warning: But if you dare describe this unfortunate critter as "a helpless little ball of fur," you will surely deserve the *yuks* that editors, and Peck, will give you for using the overworked cliché.

Okay, let's switch to dogs.

Most emerging writers trip on two very obvious wickets and fall flat on their manuscripts. They type a tale about rescuing Rover, who is adrift in a canoe at the brink of the Niagara Falls. Or, even worse, about courageous old Fido dashing into a burning house and carrying out a baby. Then he scoots back into the flames and brings out the fire insurance policy, wrapped in a wet towel. And telephones State Farm.

Uncle! I can't take any more.

However, I do understand you. Because there's a dog who owns you and you want the world to meet trusty old Rusty. Okay, I give up. Write it. Tell us, if you must, how you come home from work or school and there's Rusty, wagging his bushy tail, and getting sick on the rug.

But perhaps prior to your writing about dear old Spot (derivation of name deleted for reasons of taste) you'll allow me to suggest that you read the best dog story I ever met.

Its title is *Mirror of My Mood,* and the author is Bil Gilbert. It was published in *Sports Illustrated.* Also condensed in the August 1975 issue of *Reader's Digest.*

You'll need about five minutes to gulp down the entire story. Yet I suggest you take ten, because there's a lot of sacrificial wine in this little yarn that begs sipping. The crux of the story is that the man has decided to kill an aging dog that he loves.

Personally, I've never written a dog story. After reading *Mirror of My Mood* it was easy to decide that I couldn't aspire to match such brilliance.

But I put a dog in *Kirk's Law.*

In fact, there are three dogs in that novel; only two have names. The principal animal belongs to an old Vermont mountain man whose name is Mr. Sabbath Kirk. His dog he named Tool.

Mr. Kirk would keep a dog that would work. Tool seemed to fit his hand better than the handle of his ax. So the name seemed to fit the dog, like a steely ax blade. It was a name for a lean animal that could earn far more than her keep, as a huntress, guardian, and companion.

If you pen a story about an animal, real or absurd, give the beast's name ample thought. A name is part of a character.

Several years ago, I scribbled out a short story, in poetry, about a termite who couldn't stand the taste of wood. It was easy to find my termite a name. Opening the telephone directory, my finger did the walking through the white pages to W. Sure enough, there was my name: Woodruff.

Next came the story of an unbusy bee (a drone) who was too lazy to work and claimed to be allergic to pollen. I named him Beecher. Then, in the Alps, I wrote a ridiculous tale about a large and noble St. Bernard dog. He just had to be Northrup.

In a serious book, let your human talk to his animal. Usually, a man honestly believes in things he says to his dog.

Oddly enough, the best animal story I ever wrote was about an alley cat. Typical of alley cats, she had no name at all. But the book was entitled *Wild Cat* . . . for a totally wild creature whose jungle was a city.

Man and animal are not always friends.

They can also be adversaries. The best example I can think of is Ernest Hemingway's *The Old Man and the Sea*. We never get to know the giant marlin. Yet the old man, Santiago, seems to know him well; and more, he deeply respects this powerful creature on the other end of his fishing line. Santiago even talks to the marlin.

In my opinion, generally speaking, the best animal characters are those the author wisely allows to remain totally animal.

What does all this mean?

(137)

It means beware of anthropomorphizing.

That's just a literary term critics use to point out (rarely in praise) that the author has attributed human traits to his beast.

Humanizing an animal in a *serious* book is an insult to him. So please permit me to urge you not to do it. Rover, if he has any wit at all, wants to be exactly what God intended him to be, a dog. Like every living thing in Creation, he is already perfect.

A bit of advice. *Use* your animals. Let your workhorse pull a plow, and take your coon hound hunting. Let your cat catch a mouse or a bird.

In short, naturalize your animal. Do so and you'll succeed in stroking the long silky fur of your reader. He'll purr.

Love is making the effort to know someone else. It is not training that other being to become more like you. To use an old Vermont expression, "Leave be."

Nothing matures a writer more than sophistication, which is not subscribing to *Town and Country*, but rather becoming deeply acquainted with all forms of your living fellows. To narrow it all down, listen to people who do hard outdoor work to earn their bread. If you're lucky, they may share their lore with you.

I'd hiked a long way into the Florida everglades one time and was fortunate enough to meet a wise old gentleman whose name was Ed Nocker.

Ed was dumping a mixture of acorns and corn mash onto the ground. I asked him why. He told me that he planned to capture a herd of wild pigs. A day earlier, I'd seen those pigs, tusks and all. Amazed, I begged him to tell me how he'd ever do it.

"Easy," said Ed. "I just git 'em lazy enough to depend on me. Soon as that happens, they're slaves."

In awe, I stared at him, knowing that this was one of the few truly profound philosophical statements that I would ever hear. Ed knew life. He knew that animals could behave like humans. I promised myself to write about him, someday, in a book.

But I won't send him a copy. Ed Nocker can't read. My book would insult him.

Folks like Ed will help you write nifty stuff.

He's wild and free and nobody's slave. To offer him welfare would offend him. Mr. Nocker is someone to respect because he respects himself. I hope, to help my own writing improve, I meet and learn from a lot more people like Mr. Nocker.

Meet enough Eds and you're educated.

Okay, I know what you're thinking. In one breath, I warned you not to anthropomorphize; then, I turn around and admit, via Ed, that pigs can sometimes behave like people. Which proves that maybe you ought to be reading Ed Nocker's book instead of mine.

It also indicates that there are very few absolutes (rules) in writing fiction.

Why did I include the Ed Nocker anecdote in this chapter? Because it proves my earlier point. Readers get to know a character by observing his relationship to an animal. Needless to say, this animal-human link is not the only method to achieve solid characterization. It is just one way.

Had I talked to Ed about only the weather, you wouldn't know him quite as well or as deeply.

Writer's block infects people who know only people like themselves.

It's my guess that there are armies of folks like Mr. Nocker who live in America, many quite near where you live. If you've ever rolled a clean white sheet of paper into your Underwood and then stared blankly at its blankness for a half-hour, it's because you haven't yet met Ed. Right now, as I write this chapter, I'm in agony because I'm itching to tell you more about him.

I want to tell you how he cooked squirrel and possum. How he built a simple box-trap to catch a coon. I long to share with you his recollections of a mule, Esme, he once owned. He'd taught his mule, on command, to lift up her right-front hoof and shake hands.

But I won't.

Now then, if you want to write a book that deals only with animals, fine and dandy.

However, please remember that you, I, and all of our readers live in a world of both animals and humans.

What I'm saying is this:

Humans only, or animals only, would never have made *A Day No Pigs Would Die* the success it is. If you read the book, my guess is that you'll heartily agree.

So I guess to write the complete story of a human being, a citizen of our world, you have to squeeze a critter or two in there somewhere. Oh, you don't really *have* to. Still, animal presence is a useful spice when you're cooking up a character.

I'll share a secret with you.

It is a trick I use, again and again, to populate a scene in a novel. The trick is a trio. It's three entities. An older person, a child, and an animal. If you've read my novels, you already know this to be true, and you've seen how it works.

Sometimes the animal is present only in spirit. For example: Rob Peck, Mr. Ed Nocker, and a dead mule named Esme. Ed, you see, showed me her harness and the plow she used to pull for him. He'd sweat at one end of that plow while his mule sweated at the other. So, in a way, I had me the pleasure of meeting Esme, even though she was dead. Ed Nocker's voice softened a bit when he talked about her.

For certain, as that old man, who lived alone in a Florida outback, told me about his mule, my heart softened a bit too.

As I advised you earlier, use your animals. Let them work and earn their keep. Strange, but the dead mule didn't really *live* for me until an old man walked me to his shed to show me her plow and her harness.

Right now, I'd bet that you and I could sit down together, as friends, lean our backs against two neighboring trees, and chat for at least a day about the animals we now have or once had. The pair of us might even miss supper.

Maybe that's the way it ought to be between you and one of your readers.

What I want you to look for, and be aware of when it happens, is that sudden magnetic pull that marries a human being to an animal. You won't need a Peck to tell you when it blossoms. It'll just pop, like corn. It will be a feeling that will dance your heart like a down-home fiddle.

Take a walk in the country and across a lonely field to an old and empty barn, one that once held animals. Imagine them still to be there. Then add the farmer and his children who tended them, worked with them, and ached with them when the work-day sun quit.

Do you want to be a writer? If so, then ask yourself one easy-to-answer question: "How long has it been since my hand has touched a cow?"

Go touch her.

24
Carrie Nation and the Vigilantes

I don't remember Carrie Nation.

However, lots of our senior friends do. Back around 1918, she was a vigilante. Carrie was a little old lady who invaded saloons, raked her umbrella along the mahogany, and smashed bottles of booze.

Carrie hated drinking because a lot of innocent children were cold and hungry as a result of tippling fathers.

She became an American heroine.

To her way of thinking, vigilantism was the only answer, and maybe she was right. We'll never know. Anyhow, I cracked a Webster and here's the definition I found:

Vigilantism is "the summary action resorted to by vigilantes" when law fails.

Today, all we have to do is read the papers to realize how law, lawyers, judges, and our courts *fail* to put away the punks who want to damage nice folks.

I'd love to be a vigilante.

My first act would be to grab my umbrella—better yet my biggest ax—invade an electronic video saloon, and demolish Astro Blasters.

If I get angry enough, or love American kids enough, I'm going to become one.

If you're serious about becoming a writer, know this. A vigilante is one jolly good character for your book.

Warning: You'll probably run into boobs, the breastworks of ignorance, who will tell you how naughty vigilantes are. They'll say vigilantes are no more than a lynch mob . . . which makes about as much sense as saying electricity is a thunderstorm or that heat is a volcano. Heat and electricity are also useful.

I'd like to think there's still an ornery old Carrie Nation in our national guts.

If not, then at least let a Carrie be a character in your story. A vigilante, as I see it, is a good guy who gets good and mad because some louts are doing lousy things to gentle people. Worse yet, to children.

"O dearie me," the hand-wringer or jack-knee in your book may wail. "We musn't take the law into our own hands."

"Hogwash," another of your characters may reply. "That's the trouble. We've let the law *out* of hand. We let *experts* decide for us. Law doesn't belong to courts and judges. It belongs to *people.*"

Now then, what do you write about that will produce one nifty novel?

My advice is, write about some adults who are preying on kids. If such a pithy issue doesn't steam you up and surge your juices, then maybe you don't give a hoot about folks, and fiction is not for you. Go be a manicurist. Or a lawyer.

Want a slogan? *Get mad and get published.*

Writing is a pig-simple craft. Most of it is horse sense. Ergo, the situation that boils *your* blood will also bubble a reader's. Injustice is the key.

Another Warning: Beware of self-pity. By that, I mean this: Do not allow your hero to feel sorry for himself because Bruno Bully has dealt him dirt. Instead, your hero, to be respected by readers, must be fuming because he's witnessed Bruno picking on a third party.

(143)

A hero cares about folks other than himself.

As every issue has two sides—and I do mean every—let's flip the coin over and bring in a bit of balance. A balance of Nature.

No one can legislate morality. All societies try and fail. Carrie Nation helped bring Prohibition, but that too was poured down the drain with Repeal. There's no way to follow the foolish fellow around in order to fence him away from folly. Give a fool a fin and the two are soon parted.

It is neither my duty nor my privilege to tell adults such as Filbert Fool how, or how not, to spend his money. If we are to have a free America, then it means freedom for all of us fools, Filbert and me.

However, where children's physical, mental, and spiritual safety is concerned (and this is very mooty ground), it is we adults who must at least consider being mother hens. To wit, we must stop our cars when a school bus stops. Kids often dart. Ergo, upon big shoulders and not little ones rests the accident-prevention responsibility.

A wit once remarked that he was neither for nor against apathy. Which may mean, to quote another philosopher, "The forces of evil take over when too many good people do nothing."

Now then, in your book, if all the good people do nothing, you won't be spinning a colorful yarn. Something's got to *happen!* Carrie must swing her umbrella and shatter a bottle of Swell Old Swill.

An ax must smash Beeper Battle.

Whose ax? Does it belong to Touchdown Terwilliger, the town hero? My guess, as a writer, is no. I think your best shot is having a quiet little nobody do it.

Lester Lump does it.

Using his trusty old Boy Scout hatchet, he marches quietly along the mall, enters the video-game saloon, and reduces Moron Mayhem into tiny pieces. Are his children there? No, Mr. Lump, the assistant village clerk, is a bachelor who lives with only a cat.

(144)

Give the cat an heroic name, like Wilburforce.

Needless to say, the law and the police and the judges, because of Lester's act, suddenly get terribly involved. Don't they always whenever it's too late? These august forces inform our good Mr. Lump that he can't do things like this.

Lester says that scum can't do things like *that*, meaning Video Vile, to the children of his town. If they do, then they'll have his ire to reckon with.

Mr. Fido Fastbuck, the proprietor of the parlor, wants to press charges. Or does he? Maybe, he second guesses, no publicity for his illicit establishment would be better. His financial backer, Moe Maffia, will replace the smashed machine with few questions asked.

In short, vigilantism will always ride in like a handsome hero *when law fails*. A little noble vigilante, not too fancy, yet fine, cooks up a dandy do. No cop, no lawyer, no court that ever existed will ever be able to squelch this urge among us common folk, to avenge a wrong.

Rest in peace, Miss Nation.

25

Law in Three Flavors

No, not vanilla or chocolate or strawberry.

If you are to become a professional writer, and a good one, this chapter is going to help guide your feet along the path. Why? It oddly enough concerns itself with a faith with which you already have been blessed.

As citizens in today's United States, we exist in an atmosphere fouled by law.

Flavor number one is *civil law*.

This type of law is enacted by groups of legislators, mostly old lawyers, who enact so much of it that they never know when to stop.

Law schools abound.

More college grads are entering law school today than ever before. Good news? Hardly. Because it seems that as the number of judges and lawyers rise, so does crime. Americans would be much better off if we closed down all the law schools for the next twenty years.

Moving on, we shall now present our second flavor with a few good licks.

Flavor number two is *Canon law.*

Church laws, like civil laws, have for centuries been yammered out by bunches of old men.

These toothless tigers have envisioned themselves as prophets. God speaks directly to them, and they then tell the rest of us lowly folk how we're to behave.

Third, there is the only flavor of law that matters.

It is *God's Law,* and a good writer respects it.

The nifty thing about Natural Law is that nobody has ever had to bother to write it down.

Growing up on a farm, as I did, a kid doesn't really have to ask a bunch of dumb questions about Right or Wrong. Luckily, it's all there to see, to feel, and to tend.

Mama and Papa, as I clearly recall, never had to *tell* us much. We were Plain People and therefore unnecessary chatter was considered frivolity. Still, I asked pesky questions, as kids do; and was told by Mama, Papa, Aunt Carrie, or my grandmother, to open my eyes and look.

They promised I'd understand.

Natural Law exists, and *acts,* so powerfully that it makes civil or canon law appear, by comparison, a tad flimsy. "Obey!" our governments and churches warn, or you'll land in Hell or Sing Sing.

To repeat somewhat, for emphasis, Nature's Law does not threaten. Instead, it *acts.*

Furthermore, it acts unencumbered by human whim or will. It merely behaves, without morality. The strong seagull snatches a fish from the beak of a weaker gull. A tall oak will spread her branches upward, her roots below, taking sunlight and water and nourishment from lesser trees.

Until a tempest topples her.

My grandmother, when I was a tadpole, led me to a pine. Reaching upward, she pulled a normal clump of five needles in order to place it upon the five fingers of my small hand. Grandmother pointed to the tree, then to me, so I would forever know that we are brothers.

Characters who follow God's Law are believable to me. They are real, as all living things obey Natural Law naturally. If not, no one will believe or read about your characters.

They'll be remaindered.

Your character, to be alive, must know that his first duty (prime law) is to himself. And to his mate, his young, and his cave.

Morality is mostly survival. All the civil and canon laws enacted, since human society unfortunately learned to speak, cannot dissuade a people from trying to keep their heads above water.

Yet morality is more than survival.

It is dream, action, success. To get ahead, Charlie will drive faster than 55. He doesn't want only to keep up. Charlie wants to *pass!*

For some uncanny reason, both civil law and canon law constantly preach *equality.*

But Nature urges *quality*. . . to aspire, to hoard like a bee or a squirrel; to dominate, as the bull of the herd.

Without such hunger there is no life.

And no novel.

Fiction is folks, which simply means that your characters must, as the friendly photographer in your family has so often and so wisely advised you, "act natural."

As an aside here, I've come to believe that teaching people how to write is merely reminding them of laws they already know. It is not a whack from my schoolmaster's rod; rather it is a kindly tap on your shoulder to pay attention, and tribute, to the world God created for us.

Life's a rugged road.

The weaklings die off, crushed beneath the wheels of my chariot as I race at a full gallop. Do I sound too unfeeling? Don't buy it. In writing this book, as well as *Secrets of Successful Fiction*, I've reined my huffing steeds to a halt, stretched down a hand, and am trying to yank you up and aboard.

There's not room in my chariot for everyone.

Perhaps only you. So, get behind me, encircle my belt with

your arms; hang on, for it is your choice whether to bump along for one heck of a wild ride or remain behind in the dust. Share the rattle of my wheels and feel the wind whip your hair.

Don't look back.

If so, you'll see the losers all shaking their fists at us, complaining. "Why doesn't *everyone* get a golden chariot?" Their protest signs will read EQUALITY.

To become a writer, one who is both professional and competent, you must *forget about equality* and sudden quick. Because neither you nor I have ever read a novel in which all of the members of a tribe were equal in brains or brawn. Nations, corporations, and families don't work this way.

Think of Natural Law as a pyramid of power and you'll be pretty much on target.

Most of human social structures are pyramidic. Lots of folks at the bottom. Few atop. The strong dominate the weak. This is God's way. Most of us, however, hover somewhere in that vast middle, neither princes nor peasants. If we're wise, we value what we have, as opposed to slavering over what we have not.

Ah! But then comes Natural Law, to whisper into ear that perhaps, just maybe, we might climb higher. One more step upward on the pyramid's incline.

So up we go.

Then we're bitten by the baronial bug. The more we get, the more we want. Again, this is Mother Nature's design. People, as well as squirrels, hoard more than they shall ever use or need.

I hope you read a book I wrote, very early in my career, entitled *Path of Hunters*.

It's about the animals that live and die in your backyard. When I observed wildlife and wrote that book, I felt about as close to the beauty and brutality of God's Law as a man could cozy. It was a righteous good feeling.

So my advice to you is this. Before you try to become a *novelist*, become a *naturalist*.

Mother God has something to teach us all; and, like so many

precious and holy things on our green and blue marble, Her lessons are entirely free. No tuition. No tepid textbooks, like the one you're now holding, written by the hand of some arrogant author who thinks *he* gave himself all of his gifts.

Make a meadow your classroom. Go at night, because the darkness is Nature's dramatic stage. Most animal life is nocturnal. Watch and learn; and cast aside the limp lessons given to you by fools like me.

Know what's so.

I still want you, however, to respect all of your teachers. Yet follow them, and me, only if we follow God. For if we fail to follow, then not a one of us merits being called Rabbi.

Why study Nature? To create characters who behave, in your pages, as real human beings. And only by the fervent study of stream and forest, and sky, will you discover exactly who you are. An analyst's couch won't point the way. Yet a child's arm, which points upward at a rainbow, will.

Which brings me to one more fascinating little adventure I wish to share with you.

Do this. Explain some natural phenomenon to a child. Keep it simple, the way God keeps it. No scientific data please, at least not on this beloved expedition. What you explain doesn't have to be Antarctica or the Grand Canyon. Let it be a bug.

Tell the child not with your mind but with your heart. Spiritual, not intellectual.

Humankind looked into a starlit sky long before it saw a library reference room or a computer printout. Empty yourself of thought, to be filled by soul. And, as your neck begins to ache from stargazing, if you feel like it, cry The child will understand.

Under starlight, one adult and one child can learn a lot of Law together. And, my friend, that is what writing good fiction is all about.

Okay, so you don't want to be a writer?

Then go to law school.

***

P.S. In 1953 I attended Cornell Law School for one long boring
      year. I was elected president of my class; and then flunked
      out, with one of the lowest scholastic averages ever re-
      corded in all of Ithaca.

26
Grady
the Greedy

Miss Agricola was tall, lean, and boring.

I remember her well. Years ago, when I was a kid in high school, Miss Agricola was my Latin teacher.

Perhaps, due to my lack of interest as opposed to her professional acumen, I never learned to palaver much Latin. However, I did labor for one entire school year, in a futile attempt to memorize her never-ending endings of irregular verbs.

At the time, I secretly imagined that her long assignments and short temper were due to a personal problem, one of acute irregularity.

Profs who teach creative writing sometimes err as did Miss Agricola. When lecturing on characterization they drone on and on about the verb *to motivate*. Motivation means absolutely zilch to you, to me, or to a yawning classroom of would-be writers. The only fact worth remembering about motivation can be mastered rather easily by briefly studying an ancient Irish king, Grady the Greedy.

King Grady knew nature and therefore he knew what folks wanted. He was the fellow who originally said, "What's mine is mine. And what's yours is . . . up for grabs."

Ask yourself, why are you reading Peck's book?

Because you want to be a success. You want to earn a home for yourself and heap up your pile. Bully for you! Because you, like Robert Newton Peck and Grady the Greedy, do *not* want your equal share of the world's land, goods, and services. You want more than your share, and Mother Nature applauds you.

"Equality" is the wail of a loser.

So, erase that E. Strive for *quality*. The first step is to understand that motivating a character is merely knowing what makes people tick, and it's good old *greed*. It is wanting.

You'll run into opposition aplenty from the sluggards who want to divvy up all the loot into equal shares. Christmas brings out the worst of them. Just about every December, someone posts me a Christmas card that features a lion lying down with a lamb.

Don't buy it.

God created lions to prey upon lambs. No man-made system of liberalism, socialism, or communism can hold a Christmas candle to divine wisdom. Political systems never work. Nature always does. I string along with God, when he said on screen (in the voice of George Burns), "I want to spend some time with the animals." So should we senders of Christmas cards.

As an emerging writer, your best shot is creating a protagonist (a hero) who wants what is not yet his. He's a hunter.

If your modern-day hero, George Grady, doesn't *want* anything, you're not going to write too grabby a novel. Furthermore, if George wants something and never attempts to grab it, your ditty is equally dull.

George Grady has to do one heck of a lot more than *covet* his neighbor's wife.

He's got to drop his binoculars, rush out the kitchen door, lean on the back fence, and accost sweaty Mrs. Miniver who resides next door and is now bending over in her un-Sanforized sun suit, troweling a radish.

"Hot diggity?" he coolly queries.

Dropping her trowel, Mona Miniver slowly rises (along

with George's Celsius), turns, and strolls leisurely over to the fence, a barrier that now seems, to George, not quite as high as his realtor and imagination had previously measured.

"Mr. Grady, I do declare. You just about frightened the pants off li'l ol' me."

Pressing against the slats of the flimsy fence, Mona's delicate fingers slowly twist a very red, very ripe radish. Ah, forbidden vegetable! George eyes it with mounting eagerness.

Right now, my dear students, I know what's uptightening you.

You're afret that I shall interrupt this enticing backyard charade and continue to preach about motivation. But, seeing as *Fiction is Folks*, I shall not be so sadistic.

Mona offers her radish through the slats; and George, with mindless abandon, parts his slavering lips for that maiden bite. He chews, swallows, as the serpents of Eden hiss in shared delight.

Yet sweet Mona's fence is still intact.

It is seven feet high and its uppermost rail is crested with barbed wire. But soft! Back in his college days, George had been a high-jumper. And a broad-jumper. However, the years and calories have not handled George's once-trim physique too lightly.

He pauses, torn by the barbs of conscience, not to mention the worry of wire. Upward he looks before leaping.

Beyond the fence awaits Mona, wife of Moose Miniver, who played defensive tackle for the Tacoma Tanks.

"Where's your husband?"

Mona blinks her green eyes, greener than the go-go lights of twin traffic signals. "Oh," she coyly responds, "he's away for three weeks. Went up to the Arctic to club seals."

George, now maddened by motivation, no longer views the fence. All he sees is Mona's beautiful beyond, a feast of forbidden vegetables, plus a rutty romp among her radishes. True, a high-jumper long ago; yet he recalls he has also been a pole-vaulter.

Sprinting to his garage, George sees his old college pole, dusty, warped with age and disuse, supine upon two supporting hooks. Pole in hand, George Grady retreats from the fence, backing slowly, measuring its barbed heights with his eyes, staring through bifocals that are still steamy from Mona's panting.

Well, enough of this story.

You're bored with it, no doubt. You aren't? Then you do agree that when a writer writes about *folks* it perks up your interest more than a lecture on motivation.

We know what George wants. He covets Mona.

Will he get her?

If you will please allow me to repeat for emphasis, just to covet is not enough.

Greed without works is dead.

The wanting, in your story or mine, must be active, not passive. A hero has to want something and then try to get his mitts on it.

Furthermore, if what George Grady desires is something that belongs to somebody else, all the better. It will heighten not only the fence but also your reader's interest.

Please remember the *fence.*

Why?

Because, dear hearts, there has to be a hurdle. You must erect a barrier between the wanter and the wanton. Or, if you prefer, between the wanter and the *wantee.*

A leggy airline hostess said that to me, in the form of an arousing question, at 32,000 feet:

"Want tea?" she coyly asked.

Overcome by admiration, I misunderstood her. I naturally assumed that she was addressing me, a wanter, and confessing that she was a willing wantee. But there was a barrier to our bliss. Hustling her to the rear of the aircraft, I discovered, despite her smiling protestations (stewardesses always smile, even during a crash) that the Necessary Room wasn't even big enough to hold one, to say nothing of two.

Back yonder, two's a crowd.

But I digress. Nevertheless, you do get the point of my vignette. The wanting isn't enough. A character must want, seek, and then be obstructed.

Let's look once again at the two major alternatives in the foregoing scenario, shall we?

1. If George desires Mona, yet he never even tries to convert his yearning into reality, we don't have a plot. And there's something else we lack: a compelling character.
2. Then, on the other hand, if Mona Miniver is too easily accessible, there is no test of George's resolute hungers. If our hero wins her as a prize, he must attain the worthy goal by surmounting and overcoming.

Plots evolve from characters.

They evolve from character weakness (lechery) as well as character strength (pole-vaulting ability). Either way, the character somehow has to be tested.

Enter the fence.

The barrier, the obstacle in George's path, performs three important functions to enhance plot and, even more important, to sharpen George's character:

1. The fence between George and Mona excites the reader.
2. The fence also, for some strange reason that all of us secretly understand, makes Mona even more enticing. Beyond its forbidding barbs, Mona's hips are more ample, her vegetation more beckoning. Her garden is greener.
3. The fence causes George to grow—in stature, in constitution, and in ways that easy access could never hope to heighten.

Hero, goal, obstacle.

Needless to say, this is not the only path of a plot. Nor is it the only method to sharpen characterization. But, in my opinion, it is the most common of all the literary devices you could ever employ.

Now then, did George ever soar over the fence on his pole? Should I bother to finish the story? I must. You'd never forgive me.

Why wouldn't you? Because lessons are only lessons, nothing more; but *fiction is folks*. You, the reader of my book, naturally realize that when people like George and Mona come into view, the reading perks with interest. It's the *people* that interest you. The folks. When you leap over the hurdle of *learning to characterize*, you'll be well received in a green garden of monetary reward.

Okay, you win.

George charges forward, aching for one more college try with his old college pole. He feels young again, fresher than when he was only a freshperson at Graffiti Abnormal. He hears a track-meet crowd cheering, a band playing the old fight song, *Go Go Graffiti*.

The fence seems closer. Beyond its heights, green pastures, greener eyes. At full speed, a rusty pole rams deeply into the soft and yielding backyard muck.

"Up," yells George Grady, recalling the immortal words of his royal Irish ancestry. "Up, up, up for grabs!"

Here, should I pause to discurse on the meaning of life? Nay. You, my reader, will not allow me to so deviate. You want to know, if you'll pardon the expression, whether or not our optimistic descendant of Grady the Greedy ascended. Did he make it?

He did!

However, only moments later, Moose stormed home unexpectedly from the Arctic (with his club) and discovered the two lovers entwined among the tendrils of his terrain.

Life is not always a bed of radishes.

27
Weasels and Theodore Roosevelt

Pampers diaper babies.

As a father of two, I can speak from experience. Thank goodness for that little sticky tab, at each diaper hip, that replaced the pin I stuck into my first child to protect my thumb.

However, don't pamper your language.

If you want a reader to respect and admire your character, let the hero speak out in plain English. Not with euphemism.

What does *euphemism* mean? It is merely a phony word used to mask, or soften, reality. For example, if little Roderick rates an F in math, he is called an *underachiever* instead of a flunk-out.

President Theodore Roosevelt, bless him, called euphemisms *weasel words*. Good old Teddy thought them to be either phony or dishonest and so do I.

Today, weasel words abound.

The garbage man is now a *sanitation engineer*. Your mailman is a *letter carrier*. A dog pound has become an *animal welfare station*. Poor folks are *the disadvantaged*. Old folks are *senior citizens*.

My father, Haven Peck, killed pigs for a living.

Today, when reviewers write about my past, they describe Papa as a man who worked at *pork processing*. Even though Haven Peck was a Vermonter who didn't smile every year, I believe this term would have bent him a grin.

Have we Americans grown so weak, so puny, that we can't come right out and speak, or write, about painful realities? Your reader wants real folks thinking and saying and doing real things. If your character, Charlie, unfortunately lost his job, please don't tell your reader that he's been terminated. Charlie got fired. He was a busboy, not a dining room attendant.

Don't weasel him.

A grown man or woman, sweating to earn an honest living, does not deserve to wrap, or warp, in diaper dialogue. So don't pamper your people or your prose.

Exception: Let's say that one of your characters is a phony. Then use your weasel words when he thinks or speaks. But not when he acts.

This won't be a problem.

If dear Reginald is a man who talks in weasel terms, it would be my guess that Reggie is rarely a man of action. Rarely is he facing an issue; usually he is running away from it. Instead of a job, he probably wants a federal grant.

Reginald is an undertaker who thinks he's a *funeral director.*

Or, if Reg is a farmer, he doesn't stroll each morning to his cow barn. He goes to his *milking lounge*, wearing designer jeans. In high school, he didn't hit well enough to make the baseball team. But he sat in the dugout as the *bat dispenser.*

Absurd?

Quite. Obviously, I strayed a bit far to prove a point. Yet if you listen up, watch TV, or read current urbane magazines, you'll notice how weasel words abound.

One of the reasons I somehow, and with lots of good luck, became a successful writer is this. I managed to crawl out of the jargon pit.

Jargon is code language that doctors write on prescriptions, lawyers write into wills, and educators write into applications for federal grants. Most, perhaps even all, of jargon could be replaced by straight talk.

Why do people use jargon?

The reason is obvious. They want to *impress* someone. So they'll gussy up a simple term, one that all of us understand, and replace it with some lengthy load of jargonese that is about as clear as if it were Japanese.

People who use jargon think that if they use enough of it, their incomes will increase.

They reason that conversation is *not* meant to be understood. Instead, talk is a blimp, one they pump full of meaningless gas, hoping that it will rise, thereby lifting them above the heads of their fellows, so they will soar upward into the heavenly levels of income, power, and renown.

These people, for some odd reason, will always be eager to make speeches. Even though, to the bewildered audience, they might just as well palaver in ancient Egyptian.

I advise you, if you aspire to becoming a successful author, not to use jargon at all. With that one exception. If one of your characters is some educational administrator, one who serves no earthly purpose but must constantly try to justify his title and salary, let him euphemize away. His language will exhibit his total uselessness.

Today, in the public school systems of America, teachers are starting to sweat. They are curious to learn why private schools are springing up everywhere; and more, they are worried about their own survival.

Well, in my opinion, if the public school network dies, it will be because administrative jargon killed it. Or bored it to death

"Why," you may be asking, "should an educator's standards be higher than a lawyer's or a doctor's?"

The answer is simple. Because teachers are the leaders of our children. Besides, so many of us enjoy resenting doctors and lawyers. But, we love to revere a teacher. When we speak of that special teacher we had, our voices soften.

We dedicate our books to her. I do.

Personally, I have dedicated books to at least half a dozen of my teachers. Not a one to a lawyer.

A long time ago, in a one-room school house, a lady by the name of Miss Kelly taught all of us for many a year, without using even one weasel word. She was not only the finest teacher I ever knew; Miss Kelly was also one of the very finest ladies.

So, except for Reginald (your phony), my advice to you is to avoid weaseling. If you don't believe me, even though I am at this moment your teacher, let's study the teachings of the greatest teacher who ever lived.

Jesus of Nazareth.

Why are the simple lessons of this ancient rabbi so enduring?

Many reasons. But one reason, from this writer's point of view, is because Jesus did not use weasel words. He taught in humble terms and used the simple units of life. Bread loaves, fishes, a camel passing through the eye of a needle.

A mustard seed.

For most of his brief life, Jesus was not a scholar. He worked as a carpenter.

His closest friends were not the learned. Not the Pharisees, or Sadducees; nor were they the intellectuals. They were Galilean fishermen whose shirts were stained from sweat and the salt of the sea. Somehow I picture Simon as a big, brawling, barrel-chested brute of a man. I hear the songs Simon sang and the jokes he told, robust and bawdy.

Simon was as real as rock.

The acid test of a brilliant mind is the ability to simplify. Ironically, simpletons complicate. If you doubt me, attend a meeting with a bunch of fools. Some idiot will always say, "This is a complicated issue."

At that point, I'm usually tempted in my blunt manner to blurt out, "I'm sure it is, to *you*."

Never yet have I seen a complicated issue. Most of the problems in your life, and in the lives of your characters, are pig simple. The rub comes in forcing ourselves, and our fictional heroes, to face the simple problem and muster the guts to apply the necessary ointment.

Work is usually the solving salve.

Why? Because it is lack of work that fosters the flunk-out, the underachiever, and federal funds.

Or the shame of honest work that has prompted our bureaucratic society to label the illegal Mexican wetback as, get this, an "undocumented person."

Could an "undocumented person" be one of your fictional folks? No. But Pancho could.

I envision Pancho, sneaking over the Rio Grande in the dark to find work. Pancho, thank the goodness, will never know that he is an "undocumented person." I, for one, shall never tell him.

Just as you are a writer, Pancho is a character. A real one. He wouldn't know a weasel word if he tripped over it. Hovering at society's bottom rung, Pancho lives in tune with Nature's infinite symphony, escaping Mexico and statistics.

And he's probably a lot happier than the bureaucrats who won't sleep a wink until they document him.

Maybe tonight, he'll sneak back home, get drunk, sing a song, make love, and sire another little Pablo.

For describing Pancho thusly, I'll be branded as being about as compassionate as Hard-Hearted Hannah. True enough, as my interest here is in my work, yours, and not Pancho's.

Looking on the bright side, if his little Pablo turns out to be cream, he will rise. Cream always does. I knov.

As a lad I spent mornings in a milking lounge.

28
Meadows or Prison Walls

Before you settle too comfortably in the glowing confidence that your characters are so wonderful, so shining, so devilishly brilliant . . . a word of warning.

Editors are folks, too.

Because of that fact, I now include this important chapter. Here's why:

A page has to be as charming as a character.

In fact, a page *is* a character. Every page of your manuscript must not only read well; it must also *look* inviting. I will now remind you of a natural phenomenon that you already know, yet have possibly ignored. As you read this chapter, check the *appearance* of your manuscript and then apply the following criterion to it.

To bolster my open-meadow philosophy, I'll ask you to revert momentarily to your own childhood and apply a basic standard that you, as a very young reader, applied with rigidity.

I ask you to do this for one specific reason. *Editors are folks*. They, like the rest of us, used to be children. Like the rest of us folk, an editor behaves and reacts, I have learned, more like a human being than a machine. So does her eye.

For this, I am grateful.

Editors not only *used* to be kids. They still are! You and I still are. So, here's the meat of the message:

Remember when you were a kid?

Miss Rulerwhack, your seventh-grade teacher, marched you to the library, commanding that you select a book to read, on which to write a report. You knew her intentions were for your own good.

Do you recall standing and leaning against some towering shelf, flipping through a book with a faded green cover that Mrs. Hush, the librarian, kindly handed you, staring at the countless pages of print? Yet, as you did so, you were making a snap decision. Did the tome tickle your interest?

What would sway your verdict?

One feature. It was this: If every page of text looked like one massive block of type, with no conversation, or small paragraphs to let in a breath of refreshing white space, your little mind (like mine) judged the book to be dull and boring. Far too wordy to fit into your weekend schedule of baseball, a cowboy matinee, and then playing Doctor with Alma Available.

Know what? You were right!

Doggone near every emerging writer, whose stuff my eyes instinctively flinch away from, has handed me page upon page upon page that looks about as inviting as a close-up view of a prison wall.

"No!" such a page yells.

Textbook authors who try to teach by composing page-length paragraphs have perhaps done more to discourage education than the frowns of Mr. Chips.

A page is an art form. So *design* your pages of text to be open, like a meadow. Not a prison wall.

Like the sweet curves of a nude, Lady Page should appear graceful, *open;* and most of all, slyly inviting. She softly beckons. "Read me, tiger. I'm ready."

Lady Page must have a profile.

If she's all solid type, built like a cement block, no reader will woo her favors or drool to taste her secret delights. She must never look like all of the other women in the world—meaning, in the book. She should present herself differently from the other page lady who stands beside her. *Open,* like a flower awaiting a sweet-tongued bee.

"Come," she whispers.

"I can't *wait!*" I reply.

In brief, if Lady Page openly displays to me her alluring contours, my roving eye cannot help but look her up and down. More than harken to her most intimate words, I'll even read between her lines.

"What I'm telling you, *re* page appearance, is not some earthshaking Peck revelation. All it be is common sense. *Open* your page. Let's look at it anew.

Imagine you're planning a party. This wingding you are about to throw is going to be the bash of the year. You can't quite decide whether to invite friends you like or people you're itching to impress. So you invite just about everyone to your party. You pour heart, soul, and gin into preparation.

On party night, your mat at the front door, like all doormats, has one word on it. However, instead of WELCOME, your doormat reads SCRAM.

No, it doesn't make sense.

Yet this is precisely what inexperienced authors do. What else do they do? They wonder why they don't get their unopened pages published. And the excuses they moan for failure are far more creative than their manuscripts:

"I live so far from New York."

"Editors today just want trash."

"But I don't have an agent."

Fiction is folks, yes, but that means folks outside your pages as well as in—readers and editors. They have normal eyes, exactly like yours or mine, that look at a prison-wall page, which is one giant, unrelenting paragraph, and it's too monstrous a task. Reading even one prison-wall page would be more a chore than trying to dice up Moby-Dick for the cat.

How do you *open* a page? How do you sculpture a cold block of marble into a shapely Venus?

How does a writer avoid building a prison wall and instead zap in a picture window that invites a reader's eye, not to mention an editor's, to gaze placidly upon an open larkspur and lily-littered meadow?

Easy:

1. Write short paragraphs. But *vary* the length.

2. Include some dialogue. Flip through *Secrets of Successful Fiction*, this book, and my novels for adults as well as for youngsters. See how I do it.

3. Even when your heroine, Melissa Maudlin, is alone, steeping in self-pity, because Rick Rover, her recent romeo, has scampered off with Wanda Wetrag, a fox he met at the car wash . . . let her talk aloud. In quotes.

"Short paragraphs and dialogue are easy," you say. "Number Three is a problem."

No, it isn't.

Even when people are alone, in a pensive mood, they speak aloud. I talk to Sarah, our cat, who, as I'm writing this very sentence, is curled up close to my boot.

Folks talk to plants.

They'll cuss the lid off a new pickle jar that won't open. Or a button that pulls off a blouse.

Dingaling!

The telephone rings. Melissa's heart leaps for JOY as she rushes to the sink to grab her bottle of dishwashing liquid. Or, her confusion solved, she answers the phone. Is it Rick? No, it's only a man who wants to sell her aluminum siding with a special bonus offer, a six-month trial subscription to *Pit Dog*.

Spatial variety cannot ensure that your page makes interesting reading. But at least it will look invitingly open.

People are kids who got bigger.

Most of your potential readers, today, grew up not in an era of print but in front of a *screen*. Librarians, rightly or wrongly, are often called *media specialists* because they've been AV'd (audio visualed).

This is the Age of the Picture.

Yet we all want our kids, as well as the adults we hire, to be able to *read*, *comprehend*, and *expound* upon what they've read. But if we who write cram our pages with words, we only defeat our intentions.

Besides, it's rude.

"Scram" isn't too polite a word to holler at your neighbor. Writing is a social business. It's a craft. Writing, even though I rapture in doing it, is how I earn my bread. Ergo, as a businessman, I respect the *law* of the buyer-seller relationship—one of manners.

A salesman must be more polite than his customer.

Let's pretend I'm selling Fuller brushes. I ring the bell. Housewife answers the door. I hold up a brush, and say, "Here you are, Stupid . . . a brush to spruce up your shabby little shack."

Bristling, she slams the door on my foot.

Undaunted, I ring again. Once more the door opens. "Say," I ask, "aren't you Melissa Maudlin?"

"Yup, I'm her."

"You used to live on Elm Street," I say. "Then you ran off to Hollywood, right after you were Miss April Bunny in the 1975 *Playpen*. I remember you. As kids we used to play Doctor, over behind the car wash, until your daddy caught us and told me to scram."

Looking shyly down, I see WELCOME at my feet.

Taking me tenderly by the hand, she leads me inside, closes the door, bolts it, and then together we tiptoe eagerly to the sink to share JOY.

"I remember everything about you, Melissa," I continue. "And I never believed a word of that messy business between you and that cad who sold aluminum siding. The article in *Pit Dog* was a pack of lies."

Looking at me with renewed longing, she sighs.

"My life's an open page."

Okay, I hope you had as much fun reading this chapter as I did writing it. I wrote it, let me say again, for one purpose. To remind you that editors have character, like the folks in your fiction.

As a writer, you may think that you'll eventually be dealing with big, awesome corporations. Random House. Doubleday. Little, Brown.

Wrong.

These are three of my publishers. At each, I usually deal with one person, not an entire, impersonal bureaucracy. One editor, who (in every case) used to be a kid.

Fiction is folks. But if you remember that it is not corporations that read your manuscripts, and heed the fact the *folks* read your fiction, your pages and their attractive (open) appearance will win you some worthy friends. Make those pages a meadow and not a prison wall. Make them friendly to behold.

Fiction is folksy.

29
Short Story Now...Book Later

My telephone rang.

"Hello," I answered, with a brilliant flash of extemporization that always stills a caller for a full second of revering awe.

"Hyo. This'n har is *Boys' Life*," twanged a male voice. "We're a callin' yew from rot cheer in Texas, 'cuz we want choo to knock out us a short story."

My heart quickened.

I envisioned tenderfooted Boy Scouts huddled around a glowing campfire, quoting my sterling phrases to their enraptured compatriots, which would boost each boy to higher gamuts of trustworthy and reverent deeds.

"Okay," I said. "How much?"

He shot me a figure—far more than I expected, and at least triple what I'm worth. Craftily, I paused. An eager buyer, I hunched, will up his ante a buck or two. Texans afford anything.

"Up your ante," I said, a sly wink deepening the impish little creases around my piercing blue eyes.

He upped it. Peck accepted.

It took a full morning to dash off the first short story that

I'd attempted in at least a fortyear. But it wasn't a very good story, so *Boys' Life* thumbed it down.

"Ah cain't hep it," the Texas voice drawled. "Ah jus' doan lock it. Hope yore a fixin' to gif us another'n. Hear?"

I heard. Taking more meticulous pains, I wrote a better short story and titled it "Banjo." Tex bought it. "Banjo" ran in the May 1981 *Boys' Life*.

"Ah," I said, my beady (and shifty) little eyes narrowing with honest greed, "perchance yet a second golden egg awaits inside this goose." So I sent a copy of "Banjo" to Frances Foster, the delightful lady who happens to be my editor at Knopf. Could this humble little story, I asked Frances, possibly be beefed into a book? Frances read it. Then, bless her heart, she quickly telephoned me to announce somewhat promising news.

"Yes," said Frances, "it *might* be a book."

"Might be?"

"Rob, I find it a very touching story, just right for the magazine. Yet not quite full enough to be a novel. It feels like the whole middle of a book with a quick ending."

"Okay," I told her, "I'll give it a bra."

"Please don't. I don't want to see "Banjo" padded in any way. And don't strain to make it a knee-slapper."

Frances advised me to start the novel with the two boys in school. Alvin Dickinson, who tells the story, feels sorry for unwashed and unpopular Banjo Byler, sees some good qualities in Banjo that other kids miss seeing, and befriends him.

My editor also recommended that I establish more fully the personality of their teacher, Miss Crowder, a lady that young Alvin respects.

Miss Crowder gives the class an assignment to write about a famous person. They are to work in teams of two. Alvin, knowing that no other kid would dream of choosing Banjo, picks him for a teammate.

One of Alvin's hobbies is to tease his younger sister, Marybell, who begs him to tell her a bedtime story. He tells her about an old prospector, a hermit named Jake Horse, who lives up on the mountain near the old spar mine and peeks into windows at night to frighten little girls.

The next day, however, it is Alvin's turn to be scared.

Alvin and Banjo head uproad, toward the deserted spar mine. Banjo then springs his surprise. The famous person that the two boys will research and write about, Banjo says, is Jake Horse.

They don't actually find him.

Instead, they accidentally fall into a huge empty silo at the mine, injure themselves, and figure they will remain down there forever. Jake Horse comes and hauls them out. *But* I made him too friendly, too quickly. Foolishly, I ignored a few more of my editor's suggestions and mailed a first draft to New York. Eyeing it, Frances pointed out my errors, by telephone.

"Jake Horse's conversion," she said, "comes about too soon. Keep him gruff and grumpy for awhile, true to his hermit nature."

"Okay," I sighed. "Anything else wrong?"

"Plenty. Please don't make Alvin's little sister, Marybell, such a brat. Soften her personality, then harden old Jake's, and perhaps we're a lot closer."

"That's all I have to do?"

"Not quite. What you sent me looks like three stories instead of one continuous plot. In other words, what I hope you'll send me for a next draft is one novel, not three episodes."

I paused. "There seems, according to you, a lot of things wrong with it. Didn't I do *anything* right?"

"Yes," said Frances, a thousand miles away, yet almost as though she were seeing my sensitive eyes about to flood with hurt. "The way you've introduced Jake Horse with a bedtime story is brilliant. And that was a surprise that absolutely delighted me."

"Thanks," I said modestly, my voice no longer screeching with artistic indignation, returning now to its usual rich and resonant baritone.

"However,' said Frances, 'your ending's wrong. Too

abrupt. You're almost saying '. . . and, once Alvin and Banjo escaped from their fall into the spar silo, they lived happily ever after.' " She paused "What was that crack I heard?"

"Nothing," I snapped.

"It sounded like someone breaking a pencil."

"Don't be absurd," I said, trying to pry a yellow splinter of wood from my finger. "Only childish people snap a pencil in two."

"I quite agree. You're much too mature. Do you want to take a few notes? I'll hold on while you fetch another pencil."

"Don't bother," I said coldly.

"Short stories," Frances went on to cackle into my black plastic, "can end abruptly. O. Henry did it. Yet I don't want that. I want more school at the end, so I can see all the children appreciating Banjo now, plus more of Miss Crowder. She's a dear teacher so don't kiss her off the way you'd lick a gold star."

I said nothing.

"Operator," said Frances, "we've been cut off."

"No," I said. "I'm considering what you said."

"And?"

"You're right. I'm mentally writing a new ending," I said. "Not a vaudeville blackout but a slow fade, a real popcorn-selling, Kleenex-wetting, Hollywood ride-into-sunset finish. Violin music up. Perhaps even a tight shot of my artistic hands as I accept the Nobel prize for literature in Oslo."

"Stockholm."

"Is that all?" I asked.

"The best way to promote a short story into a novel," said Frances, "is to preview the elements earlier. One at a time, establish the characters of Alvin, Miss Crowder, Banjo, Alvin's mother and sister; and then whet the reader's appetite by hinting, as you did, about the mysterious old Jake Horse."

"Stretch it out, in detail, using elements that already exist, without padding in new stuff just to make it longer?"

"Right on," said Frances. "Alvin Dickinson tells your story, so let me get to *know* him. Show me how Banjo's unpopularity bugs Alvin. He mustn't just *decide* to befriend Banjo, so supply the reasons."

"Okay."

"One more thing. Establish more fully Banjo's banjo. After all, that *instrument* is what makes the boy so unique. Instead of adding extra ingredients, pump up what your short story already covers too briefly. Most important, let me see the precise differences between the two boys in personality."

What my editor told me was sound.

To benefit fully from this chapter, dig up a May 1981 issue of *Boys' Life* at a library and later read the book. Compare them. You'll see how I followed Frances Foster's helpful hints. "Banjo" became a book.

I used what I already had.

Taking the advice of my editor, I avoided a hurried splash into the pond of my plot. Instead, one at a time, I waded into the characters. The character of the boy who tells the story in first person, Alvin Dickinson, is established, as one would naturally suppose, smack dab at the opening gun of Chapter One.

Alvin was the camera who not only *looked* at the teacher, Miss Crowder, and all his classmates. He also registered his *feelings* to the reader.

Needless to say, I felt that it would be necessary to introduce Banjo as soon as possible. What I introduced was not the boy himself, but rather Alvin Dickinson's assessment of Banjo Byler and his unwashed problems.

I gave Miss Crowder a football.

Instead of just a teacher who drones to a bored class that it's time to grunt out a theme, I let Miss Crowder be a cheerleader. She held a football and chanted out the unpopular assignment as though she were parading the gridiron's sideline in a miniskirt. Allow me to add here that Miss Crowder is built more like a fullback than a cheerleader.

With specific regard to characterization for your own purposes, let me share a secret with you—one I use.

Use a chubby, enthusiastic lady.

There exists an endearing quality in a woman of extreme dimensions who, nonetheless, has undaunted spirit. To wit, the way I continue to employ Miss Boland, the enormous county nurse (in white) in my *Soup* books. Her enthusiasm abounds. The school board is usually dead-set against a project; yet Miss Boland, with her chins jiggling with resolute determination, says "We can *do* it."

In my short story, the reader doesn't really get to know Miss Crowder. She's only a prop.

Yet, when I pumped the little story into a full-blown book, our teacher came bugling forth like a cavalry charge. And, when Alvin (our hero) selects the unpopular and misunderstood Banjo Byler for a teammate (or rather a thememate) in school that day, it is Miss Crowder who adds her chubby nod of approval.

Characters are not remote islands. They are keys on a chain like the Florida Keys, they are linked together by chains and bridges of interaction.

Alvin picks Banjo as Miss Crowder, in her wisdom, blesses this unexpected union.

Reviewing my short story, I can see that I didn't fully introduce Alvin's family (or even Alvin himself) to the reader. In the book, however, I establish his mother, who foremans the family; his father, who pretends to; and his troublesome little sister, Marybell.

The term *relationship* makes me gag. It's overused and meaningless.

However, as Alvin and Marybell are *related*, being siblings, I had to express how an older brother and a younger sister *get along*. As a father of just such a pair of offspring, I'm fully vested in observation. Conclusion: They don't *get along* at all.

Brothers bully. Little sisters scream.

Not that I wanted to portray Alvin as the total rascal and Marybell as the absolute brat; yet it seemed, to me, a logical starting block. Why? Because it's so much easier to tone down two outrageous personalities instead of trying to add color and rough edges to a brace of bland ones.

Bear in mind, please, this chore is also a lot easier for editors.

Few editors, are inclined to take the time and thought to beef up a blah brother or a tepid sister.

Jake Horse, the old hermit, was a snap to characterize. And, taking my editor's advice, I resisted allowing old Jake to blossom too soon. A cactus rarely does.

Also, I needed a touch of outside humor, so I invented Doc, the cantankerous old medico who somehow, near the end of the book, can't quite believe Alvin's foolhardy adventure, and expresses his disapproval of how children behave. This he grunts out to Alvin while en route to reset Banjo's broken leg.

"Kids," Doc snorted, gunning his gas pedal. "You all ought to get cooped in a pit until you're twenty-one. Freemont don't need a school. We need a stockade."

To conclude, when augmenting a short story into a novel, do this:

1. Introduce your characters, one by one, to your audience of readers. Do *not* begin with a crowd scene, featuring all of your principals on stage or a big opening number.
2. Allow your hero (your Alvin) to digest each serving of humanity as it enters his life. Show your reader what the hero thinks and feels about each one.
3. Bring a character into your story; then yank him offstage, so that he can reappear later in the plot. This does not apply to your Alvin, who is onstage throughout the entire tale.
4. Add extra characters. But be careful to add only those whose function is directly associated with the thrust of your plot.
5. However, before adding characters and satellite events, use what you already have established in the

short story. Use it, enlarge upon it, and paint it with detailed strokes of a finer brush.

Remember, if you've written a short story—a good one—you *can* widen your screen, move in closer with your camera, and hatch another breed of bird.

A novel.

30
Last Gasp

This is the final chapter.

I'm sorry about that. Writing this book has so rapturously entertained me that I am a bit sad to wrap it all up.

This final note is to poke you in the ribs, tell you stuff you might not like, and agitate you enough to yank the dustcover off your Underwood. I want to provoke you and drag you kicking and screaming up a golden staircase to fame and fortune. It's so lonely up here at the top. I crave your good company.

Thus, I will now jot a few things I've learned by reason; plus a few more that my emotions spew out, like venom, for your ire to handle. So, to provoke you . . .

Here goes:

1. Two people recently robbed me. One, a mugger, stuck a gun in my ribs and took my money. The other, a college prof I never met, applied for a federal grant and took your money as well as mine. I respect the mugger more. At least he did his own dirty work.

2. Cost-of-living adjustments do accomplish one thing.

They continually increase everyone's cost of living.

3. "Mr. Peck," I was asked by a little girl in a mixed audience of kids and parents, "why do you write books and visit schools?"

    I told her the truth. *For the money.* It is adults, not children, who gasp at honesty.

4. Plato was no thinker. He was a Platotalitarian snob. I believe, after reading his work, that he loathed the common people and wanted them saddled with an awesome government that would set all standards. What he feared most was the potential upward mobility of a peasant like me.

5. Only idiots champion public transit. A *car* is what we want and need. It is handy, quick, on time, in our control and not a bus driver's. Best of all, a car is private. I don't want to sit beside Calvin Coldgerm, and I'll bet Cal feels the same about me.

6. Never buy anything, including religion, from anyone who telephones you. Whenever one of these pests call me, I politely ask him to hang on because there's someone at the door. Five minutes later, I hang up the phone.

7. New York City is a rotten place to visit, and no self-respecting New Yorker would ever want a red-neck like me to live there.

8. In my hands I hold an acorn and my Bible. Were I *forced* to choose only one, to cherish forever, I would pick the acorn, as it is entirely of God's making.

9. If I possess any wisdom at all, most of it was given me by a mother, father, an aunt, and a grandmother . . . none of whom could read or write.

10. America must once again learn to reward people who are bright and ambitious, instead of louts who are dirty and lazy.

11. How can we citizens tell the difference between a politician and a statesman? Easy. A politician can always

invent social programs to increase a budget and buy votes with public money. A statesman, regardless of the yaps of criticism, must find ways to cut it.

12. You can never hire brains. Only brawn. If someone is really brilliant, he or she will eventually leave your employ to build his or her own empire.

13. Almost everyone I meet in the field of education has little or no idea of how to handle money. I'm considering a book to help teachers and profs look after their loot and lire, to be entitled *Mr. Blue Chips.*

14. Please explain to me why American women (who spend billions on cosmetics, tight jeans, hairdressers, perfume, and gymnastic dancing) claim they don't want to be sex objects. I'd give anything to be a sex object, for just a day.

15. Men are smarter than women. No man would dream of buying a shirt that buttons up the back.

16. It's my observation that an Ivory Soap percentage of amateur tennis players should never have learned to keep score. Worrying about one little point causes most players to pittypat instead of *hit.*

17. There's a sign in my office. *You Must Smoke Here.* It works like a charm, for it keeps out both groups.

18. Unless you're an ignorant slob, a jury won't give you a fair trial. They are not *your* peers or *mine.* Some of them have nothing better to do than sit in a jury box and if you look bright, groomed, successful . . . they'll nail you. So serve on a jury the next time you're called. And no excuses.

19. Much of humor is memory. Jack Benny, a brilliant comic, merely established a few facts about his nature, which the audience, for decades, fondly loved to remember. If you don't believe that humor is memory, go back and read Chapters 4, 17, and 26. Little wisps of repetition make us grin.

20. If you want friends, learn where their soft spots are.

We all have them. Don't stomp on someone else's; tip-toe graciously around it, and never let him know that you're aware he has one.

21. I have only one recurring nightmare; that being, someday my talent will fail and I'll have to go back to killing hogs. I hated that job. All the men I worked with did, save one. Him I pity more than any man I have ever known.

22. My dearest pal on Earth is probably Fred Rogers, the famous Mister Rogers on television. We disagree on every issue. Yet no disagreeable word has even passed between us.

23. I dedicate more books to *teachers* and to *librarians* than to anyone else, because, as I am a Vermonter, debt taps my shoulder.

24. Folks I admire the most are farmers. They know how to raise cabbage, calves, and children.

25. The disease of socialism could have been cured, like ham, had only the unfortunate victim (the socialist) been raised on a farm.

26. *Advice to women:* For your sweetheart, choose a man who is physically strong. If manly in all respects, he will be secure enough to be tender, gentle, delicate. Only the unproven sissy will bully you.

27. Manhood, like trees, is rooted in earth. If you are a woman and you fancy a buck who does not yet own land, beware.

28. Authors, old buildings, and retired hookers have one thing in common: If they manage to stand up long enough, they become quaint.

29. One tiny birth-control pill, properly used, accomplishes more for our beautiful planet than ten social workers or twenty environmentalists.

30. For centuries, we have hollered at our young people, "Don't make love!" Yet youngsters oddly persist in, pardon the expression, doing it. Perhaps, as adults,

we could consider not ordering the Amazon River to flow backwards. Immorality concerns me less than the spreading disease of human pregnancy.

31. Highways, humans, and cars are built today for high speeds. Therefore 55 m.p.h. is unrealistic. It isn't the brisky driver I fear. It's the drunk.

32. Moments after an accident involving two cars, the driver who yells louder is usually at fault.

33. Animals may be superior to humans because they don't wonder where they came from (evolution) or worry about where they're going when they die (salvation). They do what has to be done, and perhaps that's why we humans adore them so. We're hoping a fluffy tuft or two of creature nobility will rub off.

34. My body is my soul's cathedral. Ergo, my body is trim and tight from work and athletics; and a reddy-brown from birth.

35. Justly so, people who try so hard to get something for nothing usually end up with far less than the rest of us.

36. Old folks' homes should be given a new name, a happy haven for the frail, feeble, and senile. Perhaps we should call these homes Supreme Courts.

37. Education is not a social service. It's a commodity, like pork jowls and soybeans. Private schools now spring up abundantly because public schools have become pawns of government and courts.

38. Health is a personal matter. It is not a governmental problem that so many of us prefer our forks to exercise, smoke to fresh air, and booze over orange juice.

39. We need new prisons. They should be enclosed, colorful factories, not gray dungeons; where criminals learn a craft, produce products, and earn a decent wage. A modern prison could support itself without a penny of public funds.

40. Let's say you're successful. A slob sues you. Whether

you (defendant) win or lose, you must pay your lawyer. But if the slob (plaintiff) loses, he pays his lawyer
nothing. If he wins, you pay him and both lawyers,
yours and his, plus all court costs. Need I say more
about our decaying judiciary?

So, dear troops, that about ties my bow. I hath given you figs
from a thistle.

I've told you all I know, which accounts for three chapters,
and faked the rest. Filling my chair will not be a snap. It'll mean
hours, days, years of unpublished sweat. Yet easier for you than
for me. You're lucky.

You have a Peck to hug you.

Index

Territorial issues, 91
Thinkers, 5
Thoughts, 5, 29, 30
Tools, 60-64
Touch, 107
Toynbee, Arnold, 66
Trig, 48

V

Variety, 39
Video Storyboard Tests, 38
Viewpoint of women, 48-53

Vigilantes, 142-145
Villains, 94-99
Vinson, Soup, 13

W

Wallis, Budge, 1
War, 44-46
West, Mae, 71
Wild Cat, 137
Wilson, Sloan, 12
Women's point of view, 48-53
Work, 61; 162
Writer's Digest Books, 1, 2

Other Writer's Digest Books

General Writing Books

Beginning Writer's Answer Book, edited by Polking, et al $9.95
How to Get Started in Writing, by Peggy Teeters $10.95
International Writers' & Artists' Yearbook, (paper) $10.95
Law and the Writer, edited by Polking and Meranus (paper) $7.95
Make Every Word Count, by Gary Provost (paper) $6.95
Teach Yourself to Write, by Evelyn A. Stenbock $12.95
Treasury of Tips for Writers, edited by Marvin Weisbord (paper) $6.95
Writer's Encyclopedia, edited by Kirk Polking $19.95
Writer's Market, edited by P.J. Schemenaur $18.95
Writer's Resource Guide, edited by Bernadine Clark $16.95
Writing for the Joy of It, by Leonard Knott $11.95

Magazine/News Writing

Complete Guide to Marketing Magazine Articles, by Duane Newcomb $9.95
Craft of Interviewing, by John Brady $9.95
Magazine Writing: The Inside Angle, by Art Spikol $12.95
Magazine Writing Today, by Jerome E. Kelley $10.95
Newsthinking: The Secret of Great Newswriting, by Bob Baker $11.95
1001 Article Ideas, by Frank A. Dickson $10.95
Stalking the Feature Story, by William Ruehlmann $9.95
Write On Target, by Connie Emerson $12.95
Writing and Selling Non-Fiction, by Hayes B. Jacobs $12.95

Fiction Writing

Creating Short Fiction, by Damon Knight $11.95
Fiction Writer's Help Book, by Maxine Rock $12.95
Fiction Writer's Market, edited by Jean Fredette $17.95
Handbook of Short Story Writing, by Dickson and Smythe (paper) $6.95
How to Write Best-Selling Fiction, by Dean R. Koontz $13.95
How to Write Short Stories that Sell, by Louise Boggess $9.95
One Way to Write Your Novel, by Dick Perry (paper) $6.95
Secrets of Successful Fiction, by Robert Newton Peck $8.95
Writing Romance Fiction—For Love And Money, by Helene Schellenberg Barnhart $14.95
Writing the Novel: From Plot to Print, by Lawrence Block $10.95

Special Interest Writing Books

Cartoonist's & Gag Writer's Handbook, by Jack Markow (paper) $9.95
The Children's Picture Book: How to Write It, How to Sell It, by Ellen E. M. Roberts $17.95
Complete Book of Scriptwriting, by J. Michael Straczynski $14.95
How to Make Money Writing . . . Fillers, by Connie Emerson $12.95
Confession Writer's Handbook, by Florence K. Palmer. Revised by Marguerite McClain $9.95
Guide to Greeting Card Writing, edited by Larry Sandman $10.95
Guide to Writing History, by Doris Ricker Marston $9.95
How to Write and Sell Your Personal Experiences, by Lois Duncan $10.95

How to Write and Sell (Your Sense of) Humor, by Gene Perret $12.95
How to Write "How-To" Books and Articles, by Raymond Hull (paper) $8.95
Mystery Writer's Handbook, edited by Lawrence Treat (paper) $8.95
Poet and the Poem, revised edition by Judson Jerome $13.95
Poet's Handbook, by Judson Jerome $11.95
Sell Copy, by Webster Kuswa $11.95
Successful Outdoor Writing, by Jack Samson $11.95
TV Scriptwriter's Handbook, by Alfred Brenner $12.95
Travel Writer's Handbook, by Louise Purwin Zobel $13.95
Writing and Selling Science Fiction, by Science Fiction Writers of America (paper) $7.95
Writing for Children & Teenagers, by Lee Wyndham. Revised by Arnold Madison $10.95
Writing for Regional Publications, by Brian Vachon $11.95
Writing to Inspire, by Gentz, Roddy, et al $14.95

The Writing Business

Complete Handbook for Freelance Writers, by Kay Cassill $14.95
How to Be a Successful Housewife/Writer, by Elaine Fantle Shimberg $10.95
How You Can Make $20,000 a Year Writing, by Nancy Hanson (paper) $6.95
Jobs for Writers, edited by Kirk Polking $11.95
Profitable Part-time/Full-time Freelancing, by Clair Rees $10.95
The Writer's Survival Guide: How to Cope with Rejection, Success and 99 Other Hang-Ups of the Writing Life, by Jean and Veryl Rosenbaum $12.95

To order directly from the publisher, include $1.50 postage and handling for 1 book and 50¢ for each additional book. Allow 30 days for delivery.

Writer's Digest Books, Department B
9933 Alliance Road, Cincinnati OH 45242
Prices subject to change without notice.